Women
of
Sacred
Song

For Amy Louise Partner
mother, sister, grandmother, and friend

Women

Meditations on
Hymns by Women

of

Sacred

Song

MARGARET & DANIEL PARTNER

Fleming H. Revell
A Division of Baker Book House Co
Grand Rapids, Michigan 49516

Published by Fleming H. Revell
a division of Baker Book House Company
P.O. Box 6287, Grand Rapids, MI 49516-6287

Printed in the United States of America

Library of Congress Cataloging-in-Publication Data

Partner, Margaret, 1948–
    Women of sacred song : meditations on hymns by women / Margaret & Daniel Partner.
        p.   cm.
    Includes index.
    ISBN 0-8007-5700-9
    1. Hymns—Devotional use. 2. Christian women Prayer-books and devotions—English. I. Partner, Daniel. II. Title.
    BV340.P37   1999
    264'.23'082—dc21   99-16336

Scripture marked KJV is from the King James Version of the Bible.

Scripture marked NIV is from the HOLY BIBLE, NEW INTERNATIONAL VERSION®. NIV®. Copyright 1973, 1978, 1984 by International Bible Society. Used by permission of Zondervan Publishing House. All rights reserved.

Scripture marked NLT is from the *Holy Bible,* New Living Translation, copyright © 1996. Used by permission of Tyndale House Publishers, Inc., Wheaton, IL 60189. All rights reserved.

Scripture marked NRSV is from the New Revised Standard Version of the Bible, copyright 1989 by the Division of Christian Education of the National Council of the Churches of Christ in the USA. Used by permission.

For current information about all releases from Baker Book House, visit our web site:
http://www.bakerbooks.com

Contents

Introduction

The Bible records a long journey from paradise to paradise, from Eden to New Jerusalem. The trek begins in innocence and purity. But soon, the travelers, man and woman, Adam and Eve, you and I, are slogging through pain and curse.

In the beginning, man and woman were created in the image of God with equal responsibility and blessing (Genesis 1:26-29, 30). But they fell away from their creator. As a result, God drove them both out of paradise. "And at the east of the garden of Eden he placed the cherubim, and a sword flaming and turning to guard the way to the tree of life" (Genesis 3:23).

The journey had begun.

And here we are today—a long way down the road from Eden. God has come as the Son, was crucified to accomplish redemption, and went away, his work complete. But in Christ's resurrection God is with us always as the Spirit. We are redeemed to God, freed from the curse. Although we were once cut off from the fruit of the tree of life, God has given us Jesus Christ, the bread of life, as our real food.

This is the gospel, and it begins with a young woman through whom God initiated his incarnation in Jesus. Her name is Mary.

Many women follow. Some are known; most are unknown. Women like those who traveled with the Lord and provided for all the disciples out of their own resources (Luke 8:1–3); the woman who anointed the Lord's body before his burial (Matthew 26:6-13); and those who watched as Jesus was crucified (27:55–56), sat nearby as he was buried (v. 61), and were the first to return to the empty tomb (28:1). During the wait in Jerusalem for the promise of the Father, the women were there praying with the eleven disciples and the Spirit descended upon them all (Acts 1:13–14). Tell the story of these women and you tell the gospel.

The church age is the passage of nearly two thousand years of innumerable people loving God. We know the names of few of these believers. Least of all do we know the women. Yet their work must not be underrated.

Mary Elizabeth Braddon, the nineteenth-century British novelist, wrote, "Women are the church's strong rock. As they were the last at the foot of the cross, so they have become the first at the altar."

At that altar, you can hear them singing.

Which is a reason we made this collection. Christians love to sing and women have made marvelous gifts to the musical literature of the church. The fifty hymns gathered in this book are a portion of this treasure.

Why do we sing? For worship of God? Yes. Praise of the Lord? Yes. And the apostle Paul gives another reason: "That Christ may dwell in your hearts through faith, as you are being rooted and grounded in love" (Ephesians 3:17). So he urges us to "be filled with the Spirit, as you sing psalms and hymns and spiritual songs among yourselves, singing and making melody to the Lord in your hearts" (5:18–19). Therefore we present this book of hymns to you in hope and prayer that your love for God will grow.

These hymns are rich in spiritual meaning; they were enjoyed by generations past, yet are fresh today. This enabled us to write a short thought to accompany each hymn. These thoughts are like peaches picked from a ripened tree. So much is sweet and nourishing here—a taste of the truth of the gospel. We pray that this fruit will edify the saints and in some modest way help to build the church.

The grace of our Lord Jesus Christ be with all of you.

Margaret and Daniel Partner
June 1999

Nearer, My God, to Thee

Nearer, my God, to thee, nearer to thee!
   E'en though it be a cross that raiseth me;
Still all my song would be, nearer, my God, to thee,
   Nearer, my God, to thee, nearer to thee.

Though like the wanderer, the sun gone down,
   Darkness be over me, my rest a stone;
Yet in my dreams I'd be nearer, my God, to thee,
   Nearer, my God, to thee, nearer to thee.

There let the way appear steps unto heav'n:
   All that thou sendest me in mercy given;
Angels to beckon me, nearer, my God, to thee,
   Nearer, my God, to thee, nearer to thee.

Then, with my waking thoughts bright with thy praise,
   Out of my stony griefs Bethel I'll raise;
So by my woes to be nearer, my God, to thee,
   Nearer, my God, to thee, nearer to thee.

Sarah Flower Adams (1805-1848)

Born in Essex, this daughter of publisher Benjamin Flower, who was once imprisoned for criticizing the Bishop of Llandaff, married William B. Adams, an engineer and inventor, in 1834. In 1837 Adams appeared as Lady Macbeth at the Richmond Theatre in London in a successful production of *Macbeth*, but she found the work so strenuous that she gave up the stage to continue her writing. Her enduring hymn has appeared in many hymnals, and its popularity continues to this day.

The Book of Genesis is full of significant events. One is Jacob's journey to Paddan-aram. There he would find and marry his wives, Leah and Rachel. Along the way "he arrived at a good place to set up camp and stopped there for the night. Jacob found a stone for a pillow and lay down to sleep" (Genesis 28:11 NLT). Here today's hymn begins.

"As he slept, he dreamed of a stairway that reached from earth to heaven. And he saw the angels of God going up and down on it" (v. 12). Verse three of Sarah Adams's hymn interprets this stair as signifying the way to God. Each step is an experience of life sent by God, like angels drawing us nearer.

"Then Jacob woke up and said, 'Surely the LORD is in this place, and I wasn't even aware of it'" (v. 16). As he slept on that hard stone, Jacob encountered God, who retold the promise made to Abraham (see vv. 13–15). This awakened Jacob. The stony grief of life can wake you up too. In it you encounter God and the promises of the gospel.

"The next morning [Jacob] . . . took the stone he had used as a pillow and set it upright as a memorial pillar. Then he poured olive oil over it. He named the place Bethel—'house of God'" (vv. 18–19). What is the ultimate purpose of all this? Is it simply to bring you nearer to God? To enhance your individual spiritual life? No. Jacob named the place Bethel, which means *house of God*.

The purpose of our knowing God in Christ is that God will have a dwelling place. Remember when Peter said to Jesus, "You are the Messiah, the Son of the living God" (Matthew 16:16)? Jesus responded, "This revelation is the rock upon which I will build my church" (v. 18 paraphrase). The more you know Christ, the more Christ builds the church—the house of God.

RELATED SCRIPTURE READING—*Revelation 21:3-4*

Dear Heavenly Father, though my life's journey may become like Jacob's—the sun gone down, darkness over me, my only rest a stone— I ask that such experiences will awaken me to your promises and that my griefs will not only bring me nearer to you but also help build your dwelling place in humanity.

11

His Are the Thousand Sparkling Rills

His are the thousand sparkling rills
    That from a thousand fountains burst,
And fill with music all the hills;
    And yet he saith, "I thirst."

All fiery pangs on battlefields;
    On fever beds where sick men toss,
Are in that human cry he yields
    To anguish on the cross.

But more than pains that racked him then,
    Was the deep longing thirst divine
That thirsted for the souls of men:
    Dear Lord! and one was mine.

O love most patient, give me grace;
    Make all my soul athirst for thee;
That parched dry lip, that anguished face,
    That thirst, were all for me.

Cecil Frances Alexander (1818-1895)

Cecil Alexander published nearly four hundred hymns and poems, most of them for children. She was born in County Wicklow, Ireland, and in 1850 married William Alexander, later bishop of Derry and Raphoe, archbishop of Armagh, and primate of all Ireland. Her hymn "All Things Bright and Beautiful" first appeared in *Hymns for Little Children* (1848). This book was so popular that by 1896 it had been published in sixty-nine editions.

There are many things that people don't understand about Jesus Christ. For example, Christ is the visible image of the invisible God. This is an important fact, because through Christ we come to know God. Here are some other important details about the Son of God (see Colossians 1:15–20).

- He existed before God made anything.
- Christ is supreme over all creation.
- Through Christ God created everything in heaven and earth.
- Everything has been created for him.
- He holds all creation together
- He is the first to rise from the dead, so he is first in everything.
- God in all his fullness lives in Christ.
- By Jesus Christ God reconciled everything to himself.

To be sure, this is not a list to be memorized. Rather, it is the description of a person whom you can love. He thirsted on the cross. He thirsted for your soul. By the blood shed as he died, God made peace with everything in heaven and on earth, including you. Join Cecil Frances Alexander today and pray, "O love most patient, give me grace; make all my soul athirst for thee."

RELATED SCRIPTURE READING—*John 6:37–38*

Jesus Christ, you are indeed love most patient. I know you thirsted on the cross for me; please give me grace that my soul would be thirsty for you. Forgive me when I sometimes leave you—the fountain of living water—and dig for myself cracked cisterns that can hold no water. Give me yourself as my living water! Then I'll never be thirsty again.

All Things Bright and Beautiful

All things bright and beautiful, all creatures great and small,
All things wise and wonderful, the Lord God made them all.

Each little flower that opens, each little bird that sings,
He made their glowing colors, he made their tiny wings.

The purple-headed mountain, the river running by,
The sunset and the morning that brighten up the sky.

The cold wind in the winter, the pleasant summer sun,
The ripe fruits in the garden, he made them, every one.

He gave us eyes to see them, and lips that we might tell
How great is God Almighty, who has made all things well.

Cecil Frances Alexander (1818–1895)

ver since the creation of the world [God's] eternal power and divine nature, invisible though they are, have been understood and seen through the things he has made" (Romans 1:20 NRSV). How can such sublime divine distinctions be seen in physical, transitory things? Is this similar to the expression of a writer in her words or of an artist in his paints? No, these things are hardly comparable to God and the creation.

God is invisible. But Jesus Christ, the Son of God, is not. As he said, "Whoever has seen me has seen the Father" (John 14:9). In fact, Christ is "the image of the invisible God" (Colossians 1:15). God cannot be seen without Christ. Yet Scripture also says that God can be seen and understood through the creation. How can this work both ways? Let's allow the Scripture to tell us.

The Gospel tells us that the Word, who was in the beginning with God, is God. Not only so, the Word is the Son of God, Jesus Christ (see John 1:1, 2, 14). And "All things came into being through him, and without him not one thing came into being" (v. 3). This means that the creation, though not in itself divine, is not independent from Christ. We can confirm this in the Epistles. "In him all things in heaven and on earth were created, things visible and invisible, . . . all things have been created through him and for him" (Colossians 1:16).

This is thoroughly mysterious yet true. Could there be a human being who has not, at least once, been awestruck at a sight of the beautiful creation? This is doubtful. Why? Because, "All things bright and beautiful, all creatures great and small, / all things wise and wonderful, the Lord God made them all"—*by* and *in* and *through* and *for* Christ.

RELATED SCRIPTURE READING—*Romans 11:34–36*

Lord Jesus Christ, you are supreme over all creation. I am in awe that through you God created everything in heaven and earth—the things I can see and the things I can't see. Dear Lord, everything, including me, has been created through you and for you. I am yours.

Our Blest Redeemer, Ere He Breathed

Our blest Redeemer, ere he
    breathed
  His tender, last farewell,
A guide, a Comforter, bequeathed
  With us to dwell.

He came in tongues of living flame,
  To teach, convince, subdue;
All-powerful as the wind he came,
  As viewless too.

He came sweet influence to impart,
  A gracious, willing guest,
While he can find one humble
    heart
  Wherein to rest.

And his that gentle voice we hear,
  Soft as the breath of even,
That checks each fault, that calms
    each fear,
  And speaks of heav'n.

And every virtue we possess,
  And every victory won,
And every thought of holiness
  Are his alone.

Spirit of purity and grace,
  Our weakness, pitying, see;
O make our hearts thy dwelling
    place,
  And worthier thee.

Harriet Auber (1773-1862)

Pierre Auber was a French Huguenot (Protestant) who fled from Normandy in 1685 when Protestantism in France became a crime. Harriet Auber was his great-great-granddaughter. This daughter of an Anglican vicar wrote her hymn for use on Whitsunday, fifty days after Easter. It was included in her book *Spirit of the Psalms* (1829), written to lift the poetry of the psalms from the stilted, unpoetical versions then in use. Some of her versions of the psalms were included in Charles H. Spurgeon's *Our Own Hymnbook* (1866) for use in his Baptist tabernacle.

While sharing the Passover supper with Jesus, the disciples became troubled (see John 14:1). Their beloved teacher was leaving! But Jesus reassured them saying, "The Father will give you someone else for comfort and counsel who will never leave you."

Who could this be? It is the Holy Spirit (see vv. 16–17 NLT).

This is good news! Imagine sitting at that table. Jesus had already told you, "Whoever has seen me has seen the Father" (v. 9 NRSV). You think, *I've certainly seen Jesus. That means I've seen the Father!* This is profound. Let's consider it.

Most Jews can recite Deuteronomy 6:4—"Hear, O Israel: The LORD our God is one LORD" (KJV). And all Christians know that there is only one God. Yet this God is a trinity—Father, Son, and Spirit. At that Passover table sat the Son, who was God and a true human being. And this man said: "My Father who lives in me does his work through me. Just believe that I am in the Father and the Father is in me" (John 14:10–11 NLT). This means that the Father and the Son are one God—undivided.

Speaking of the Spirit, Jesus said, "he lives with you now and later will be in you" (v. 17 NLT). He went on: "I will not abandon you as orphans—*I will come to you*" (v. 18, italics added). Jesus had already promised that the Spirit would come to the disciples so they would not be alone. Here the Son says that the Spirit's coming is his coming as well. What does this mean? That the Son and the Spirit are one God—undivided.

There are many reasons why our one God is three. Today's hymn tells us, ". . . his that gentle voice we hear, . . . that checks each fault, that calms each fear, . . . And every virtue we possess, and every victory won, and every thought of holiness are his alone."

RELATED SCRIPTURE READING—*John 14:15-20*

O wonderful and mysterious triune God! I thank you for who you are, even though I can hardly understand you. Thank you, Father, that you came to me in the Son. He is my Emmanuel—God with me! Thank you, Son of God, for living and dying and living again in resurrection! And thank you, Holy Spirit, that you are with me always as my comforter.

Praise to God, Immortal Praise

Praise to God, immortal praise, for the love that crowns our days;
Bounteous source of ev'ry joy, let thy praise our tongues employ:
All to thee, our God, we owe, source whence all our blessings flow.

All the plenty summer pours; autumn's rich o'erflowing stores;
Flocks that whiten all the plain; yellow sheaves of ripen'd grain:
Lord, for these our souls shall raise grateful vows and solemn praise.

Peace, prosperity, and health, private bliss, and public wealth,
Knowledge with its glad'ning streams, pure religion's holier beams:
Lord, for these our souls shall raise grateful vows and solemn praise.

As thy prosp'ring hand hath blest, may we give thee of our best;
And by deeds of kindly love for thy mercies grateful prove;
Singing thus through all our days praise to God, immortal praise.

Anna Laetitia Barbauld (1743-1825)

Reverend John Aikin became classical tutor at the dissenting academy in Leicestershire, England, when his daughter Anna Laetitia was ten years of age. This was fertile ground in which to develop Anna's gift of hymnody, poetry, and other forms of literature. With her husband, Rochemont Barbauld, a French Protestant minister, she set up a boarding school in Palgrave, Suffolk. Barbauld wrote about twenty hymns, which were published by her niece, Lucy Aikin, in *Hymns in Prose for Little Children* (1825).

Do you know how to be truly filled with the Spirit? Scripture suggests some ways: "Speak to one another with psalms, hymns and spiritual songs. Sing and make music in your heart to the Lord" (Ephesians 5:19 NIV). Christians love to sing the hymns and songs of the church. The Book of Psalms—the ancient hymnal of Scripture—is perpetually popular among us. We love to sing because we love to be filled with the Spirit. After all, the Spirit is God, and Christians love God. So we love to sing. And singing fills us with the Spirit, whom we love. What a wonderful cycle!

Ephesians continues in its instruction on how to be filled with the Spirit: ". . . always giving thanks to God the Father for everything, in the name of our Lord Jesus Christ" (v. 20). This is really practical. Most of us don't have much time for singing, but nothing prevents us from giving thanks. There is no need to shout or even speak out loud in order to give thanks to God. Try this today: Give thanks to God always for all things.

Anna Barbauld gives thanks for many things in her hymn. You may want to start your thanksgiving with them: God's love, summer, autumn, a flock of sheep, ripe grain, peace, prosperity, health, bliss, wealth, knowledge, and religion. By the end of the day you may just find yourself singing!

RELATED SCRIPTURE READING—*Colossians 3:17*

I thank you, Lord, because you are just. I give thanks because you are near. You have turned my mourning into dancing. You have taken away my sadness and clothed me with joy. I will praise you before all the people. I will give you thanks in song. O Lord my God, I will give you thanks forever!

19

Take the Name of Jesus with You

Take the name of Jesus with you,
Child of sorrow and of woe,
It will joy and comfort give you;
Take it then, wherever you go.

   Precious name, O how sweet!
   Hope of earth and joy of heaven.
   Precious name, O how sweet!
   Hope of earth and joy of heaven.

Take the name of Jesus ever,
As a shield from every snare;
If temptations round you gather,
Breathe that holy name in prayer.

O the precious name of Jesus!
How it thrills our souls with joy,
When his loving arms receive us,
And his songs our tongues employ!

At the name of Jesus bowing,
Falling prostrate at his feet,
King of kings in heaven we'll crown
   him,
When our journey is complete.

Lydia Baxter (1809-1874)

Lydia Baxter and her sister helped form a Baptist church in their hometown of Petersburgh, New York. She wrote several gospel songs, and "Take the Name of Jesus with You" continues to be sung today. Baxter's hymns were published in *Gems by the Wayside* (1855) and *Pure Gold* (1871).

ave you ever heard stories about sorcerers who use certain names as magic incantations? Do you think these names have any power? Consider the story of Elijah and the priests of Baal as recorded in 1 Kings 18. There, Elijah wanted to show Israel that God is real and Baal was nonexistent.

Elijah and the priests of Baal each had a bull to sacrifice but no fire. Elijah said to the priests, "Call on the name of your god, and I will call on the name of the LORD. The god who answers by setting fire to the wood is the true God!" (1 Kings 18:24 NLT). So the priests of Baal called on the name of Baal all day, but there was no answer (see vv. 26, 27, 29).

After drenching the wood and the altar and the sacrifice with water, Elijah prayed, "'O LORD, God of Abraham, Isaac, and Jacob, prove today that you are God in Israel.' . . . Immediately the fire of the LORD flashed down from heaven and burned up the young bull" (1 Kings 18:36–38).

So, Baal was proven nonexistent, and the people turned back to God. Does this mean that God's name contains more power than other names? Is the name of Jesus, the Son of God, a good luck piece we carry for protection? God forbid! Leave that superstition to the priests of Baal!

Jesus is the name of the man who defeated death and lives in resurrection. "Because of this, God . . . gave him a name that is above every other name" (Philippians 2:9) and, as Lydia Baxter says, this precious name is the "hope of earth and joy of heaven."

RELATED SCRIPTURE READING—*Ephesians 1:19–21*

Lord Jesus, I praise and thank you that, as the eternal God, you did not demand your rights as God; you made yourself nothing. I love you for your obedience in dying a criminal's death on a cross. Your name is above every other name. O God, speed the day when at the name of your Son, Jesus, every knee will bow and every tongue will confess that he is Lord, all for your glory.

Fade, Fade Each Earthly Joy

Fade, fade each earthly joy; Jesus is mine.
Break ev'ry tender tie; Jesus is mine.
Dark is the wilderness, earth has no resting place,
Jesus alone can bless; Jesus is mine.

Tempt not my soul away; Jesus is mine.
Here would I ever stay; Jesus is mine.
Perishing things of clay, born but for one brief day,
Pass from my heart away; Jesus is mine.

Farewell, ye dreams of night; Jesus is mine.
Lost in this dawning bright; Jesus is mine.
All that my soul has tried left but a dismal void;
Jesus has satisfied; Jesus is mine.

Farewell, mortality; Jesus is mine.
Welcome, eternity; Jesus is mine.
Welcome, O loved and blest, welcome sweet scenes of rest,
Welcome, my Savior's breast; Jesus is mine.

Jane Catherine Bonar (1821-1884)

Born near the Tweed River, Scotland, where her father was a parish minister, Jane Bonar was the wife of the famous hymnist Horatio Bonar. Her hymns appeared in Dr. Bonar's *Songs for the Wilderness* (1843–44) and *Bible Hymn Book* (1845).

"My beloved is mine and I am his," sings the maiden in the Song of Songs (2:16 NRSV). Jane Catherine Bonar echoes these words in her lovely hymn. "Jesus is mine," she says.

The Song of Songs continues its astounding scriptural account of love saying, "I sought him whom my soul loves; I sought him, but found him not; I called him, but he gave no answer" (3:1). This is a common experience of believers, seekers, and lovers of Christ. Simply put, it is the experience of *Where did he go?* Bonar probably experienced this. Have you?

John of the Cross, a Spanish Roman Catholic reformer, mystic, and poet in the sixteenth century, addressed this problem in his *Commentary on the Spiritual Canticle.* The following paraphrases his thought:

> *I sought him but I did not find him* (see Song of Songs 3:1). You ask: Since the one I love is within me, why don't I find him or experience him?
>
> Here is the reason: He remains concealed because you do not also hide yourself in order to meet and experience him. Anyone who wants to find a hidden treasure must enter the hiding place secretly. Then she will be hidden just as the treasure is hidden. To find him, forget all your possessions and all creation and hide in the interior, secret chamber of your spirit. There, closing the door behind you, pray to your Father in secret (see Matthew 6:6). Hidden with him, you will experience him in hiding; love and enjoy him in hiding. You will delight with him in a way transcending all language and feeling.

A relationship with the Lord is built on prayer. Prayer is based on love. To publicize private prayer violates the love relationship that such prayer establishes. Brag of morning prayer at noon and find that the loving God, who is in secret, won't tryst with you that night.

RELATED SCRIPTURE READING—*Psalm 42:1-3*

O God, give me grace to forget all my possessions and all the rest of creation. Show me where and how to hide in the interior, secret chamber of my spirit. I want to close the door behind me and pray to you in secret. Let me experience you in hiding; love and enjoy you in hiding.

23

Hasten the Time Appointed

Hasten the time appointed, by prophets long foretold,
When all shall dwell together, one Shepherd and one fold.
Let ev'ry idol perish: thy truth to all make known
Till ev'ry prayer be offered to God in Christ alone.

Let Jew and Gentile, meeting from many a distant shore,
Around one altar kneeling, one common Lord adore.
Let all that now divides us remove and pass away,
Like shadows of the morning before the blaze of day.

Let all that now unites us more sweet and lasting prove,
A closer bond of union, in a blest land of love.
Let war be learned no longer, let strife and tumult cease,
All earth his blessed kingdom, the Lord and Prince of Peace.

O long-expected dawning, come with thy cheering ray!
When shall the morning brighten, the shadows flee away?
O sweet anticipation! It cheers the watchers on,
To pray, and hope, and labor, till the dark night be gone.

Jane Laurie Borthwick (1813-1897)

This translator and versifier also wrote original hymns. She was
born in Edinburgh, Scotland, and, with her sister, Sarah Findlater,
published their translations in *Hymns from the Land of Luther*
(1854–62). Their original hymns were published in *Thoughts for Thankful Hours* (1857).

Ln this hymn Jane Laurie Borthwick makes an almost unnoticed reference to the Song of Songs—the series of poems that celebrate the ardent love between a king and his bride. "When shall the morning brighten," she prays, "the shadows flee away?" (see Song of Songs 2:17).

In the first century, Jewish authorities debated whether the Song of Songs should be included in Holy Scripture because it is explicit about sexual attraction. In Christian and later Jewish tradition its poetry has been interpreted symbolically. Christian expositors find in it rich symbolism of Christ's love for his church. The Song can also symbolize the love between God and the individual Christian worshiper. So sections of these love songs have found their way into Christian worship. Charles Wesley's "Jesus, Lover of My Soul" contains references to the Song as does Bernard of Clairvaux's "Jesus, the Very Thought of Thee." Here Borthwick's hymn quotes the Song of Songs in longing for the Lord's return.

"My lover is mine," sings the bride in the Song, "and I am his" (2:16 NIV). This shows the assurance of a person who loves God. But the Bible sometimes describes Christ's return in fearful terms. What expels such fear? Love. Out of love for God, the apostle Paul said, "Now there is in store for me the crown of righteousness, which the Lord, the righteous Judge, will award to me on that day—and not only to me, but also to all who have longed for his appearing" (2 Timothy 4:8 NIV). So until then let's pray like the bride: "Before the dawn comes and the shadows flee away, come back to me, my love" (Song of Songs 2:17 NLT).

RELATED SCRIPTURE READING—*Song of Songs 7:10-12*

Jesus, you are the lover of my soul; let me run to you while the storm is high. I have no other refuge but you. Please don't leave me alone. All my trust is in you, and all my help is from you. Thank you for the comfort and cover I find in the shadow of your wing.

Face to Face with Christ, My Savior

Face to face with Christ, my Savior,
Face to face—what will it be,
When with rapture I behold him,
Jesus Christ who died for me.

Face to face I shall behold him,
Far beyond the starry sky;
Face to face in all his glory,
I shall see him by and by!

Only faintly now I see him,
With the darkened veil between,
But a blessed day is coming,
When his glory shall be seen.

Face to face—oh, blissful moment!
Face to face—to see and know;
Face to face with my Redeemer,
Jesus Christ who loves me so.

Carrie E. Breck (1855-1934)

After a childhood in Walden, Vermont, Carrie Breck migrated via New Jersey to Portland, Oregon, with her husband, Frank A. Breck. She wrote many poems: "Ev'ry Prayer Will Find Its Answer" appeared in the *Baptist Hymnal* (1973) and "There Was One Who Was Willing to Die in My Stead" was published in the *American Service Hymnal* (1968). "Face to Face with Christ, My Savior" is by far her most popular hymn.

hat *will* it be like to see the Lord's face? Will we see what John saw and recorded in Revelation 1? "I turned to see who was speaking to me. . . . His head and his hair were white like wool, as white as snow. And his eyes were bright like flames of fire . . . His voice thundered like mighty ocean waves . . . and a sharp two-edged sword came from his mouth. And his face was as bright as the sun in all its brilliance" (vv. 12–16 NLT). This is Christ, the church's judge.

Will Christ be like the one John saw and recorded in Revelation 5? There John was weeping because he thought no one was worthy to open the scroll of God's eternal purpose. "But one . . . said to me, 'Stop weeping! Look, the Lion of the tribe of Judah, the heir to David's throne'" (v. 5). This is Christ, the King of the Jews. Then, strangely enough, John looked and saw "a Lamb that had been killed" (v. 6). This is Christ, the Redeemer of the world.

Later John saw a white horse ridden by a man named Faithful and True. "From his mouth came a sharp sword, and with it he struck down the nations. . . . On his robe and thigh was written this title: King of kings and Lord of lords" (19:15–16). This is Christ, the King of the earth.

How tumultuous for John to come face to face with Christ! But finally he writes, "I saw a new heaven and a new earth. . . . And I saw the holy city, the new Jerusalem, . . . like a beautiful bride prepared for her husband" (21:1–2). This is the face you will see at the end—the face of Christ the bridegroom, the husband of God's redeemed. So, "Let us be glad and rejoice and honor him. For the time has come for the wedding feast of the Lamb, and his bride has prepared herself. She is permitted to wear the finest white linen" (19:7–8).

RELATED SCRIPTURE READING—*Genesis 32:30*

Dear God, I look forward to the new heaven and new earth. Then I will see and be a part of the holy city, the new Jerusalem, like a beautiful bride prepared for her husband. So I pray for all your believers everywhere; make them, and me, ready for our marriage to you.

27

Be Thou My Vision

Be thou my vision, O Lord of my heart;
All else be nought to me, save that thou art—
Thou my best thought,—by day or by night,
Waking or sleeping, thy presence my light.

Be thou my wisdom and thou my true word;
I ever with thee and thou with me, Lord;
Thou my great Father; thine own may I be;
Thou in me dwelling, and I one with thee.

High King of heaven, when victory is won,
May I reach heaven's joys, bright heaven's Sun!
Heart of my heart,—whatever befall,
Still be my vision, O Ruler of all.

Mary Elizabeth Byrne (1880-1931)—Translator

Born in Dublin, Ireland, Byrne received her Master of Arts degree from the University of Ireland in 1905. Her treatise on England in the Age of Chaucer was awarded the chancellor's gold medal by the Royal University. She became a researcher for the Irish Board of Intermediate Education.

Eleanor H. Hull (1860-1935)—Versifier

Born in Manchester, England, Hull was president of the Irish Literary Society in London and the founder of the Irish Text Society. She wrote several books on Irish literature and history. "Be Thou My Vision" appeared in her book *Poem Book of the Gael* (1912).

his Irish poem dates back to the eighth century. Mary Elizabeth Byrne provided the church with its translation, and it was versified for singing by Eleanor H. Hull. The poem does not simply express a desire for a vision. Much more, the poet wants *Christ* to be that vision. Wisdom and truth are not enough. The poet prays that Christ himself will be her wisdom and true word.

Can Christ be these things to you? Yes, according to Scripture. He is wisdom (1 Corinthians 1:24); he is truth (John 14:6); he is the Word (Hebrews 1:2). A Christian flourishes with this sight, this view of Christ.

Peter saw it. Once Jesus asked the disciples, "'Who do you say I am?' Simon Peter answered, 'You are the Messiah, the Son of the living God.' Jesus replied, 'You are blessed, Simon son of John, because my Father in heaven has revealed this to you'" (Matthew 16:15–17 NLT). And Paul prayed for it: "I do not cease to give thanks for you as I remember you in my prayers. I pray that the God of our Lord Jesus Christ, the Father of Glory, may give you a spirit of wisdom and revelation as you come to know him, so that, with the eyes of your heart enlightened, you may know what is the hope to which he has called you" (Ephesians 1:16–18 NRSV).

Make these verses your prayer today. Bow on your knees and ask for a spirit of wisdom and a revelation of Christ. Like the ancient Irish poet, ask God to renew your understanding so you can not only see that Christ is all and in all but also live under this glorious vision (see Colossians 3:11).

RELATED SCRIPTURE READING—*Ezekiel 12:21-25*

Dear Lord, I pray not only for myself, but for the entire church of which I am a part. Don't let us be like the church in Laodicea that said she was rich and had need of nothing. We do need something, Lord: a renewed vision of you. May we find a way to buy ointment for our eyes so that we may see you. O Lord, reprove and discipline those whom you love.

29

Come and Rejoice with Me

Come and rejoice with me! For once my heart was poor,
And I have found a treasury of love, a boundless store.

Come and rejoice with me! I, once so sick at heart,
Have met with one who knows my case, and knows the healing art.

Come and rejoice with me! For I was wearied sore,
And I have found a mighty arm which holds me evermore.

Come and rejoice with me! My feet so wide did roam,
And one has brought me from afar, to find in him my home.

Come and rejoice with me! For I have found a friend
Who knows my heart's most secret depths, yet loves me without end.

I knew not of his love; and he has loved so long,
With love so faithful and so deep, so tender and so strong.

And now I know it all, have heard and known his voice,
And hear it still from day to day. Can I enough rejoice?

Elizabeth R. Charles (1828-1896)

"To know how to say what others only know how to think is what makes men poets or sages, and to dare to say what others only dare to think makes men martyrs or reformers, or both." So wrote Elizabeth Charles in *The Chronicles of the Schonberg-Cotta Family,* her novel of the childhood of Martin Luther. An Anglican, she wrote more than twenty-five books. In addition to her original hymns, she translated many from the Latin and German. Charles's hymns appeared in her *Voice of the Christian Life in Song in Many Lands and Ages* (1864), *Poems* (1867), and *Songs Old and New* (1882).

Reading the Acts and Epistles you notice that the early church had plenty of joy and rejoicing. In fact, the apostles could not stop telling about the wonderful things they had seen and heard (see Acts 4:20).

The gospel is the source of this Christian joy. For example, the jailer at Philippi was filled with joy because he had come to believe in God (see Acts 16:34). His was a basic, wonderful joy. Human life has many joys—a baby's birth, the innocence of children, the beauty of nature, and more. But none can compare with the joy in believing (see Romans 15:13).

And so Elizabeth Charles issues an invitation in her hymn: "Come and express your joy with me." One may ask, "Why?" She answers with seven reasons, one in each stanza of the hymn. But the essential reason is, "I have found a friend." Scripture phrases it thus: "Now we can rejoice in our wonderful new relationship with God—all because of what our Lord Jesus Christ has done for us in making us friends of God" (Romans 5:11 NLT).

The Philippian jailer found this basic joy when his primal loneliness, the pain of separation from God, was cured. He had found *the* friend! No doubt he joined the apostles in encouraging the church in Philippi to "rejoice in the Lord always. I will say it again: Rejoice!" (Philippians 4:4 NIV).

RELATED SCRIPTURE READING—*Acts 8:4-8*

Father, thank you for all the things for which I can rejoice. I have been made right in your sight by faith. I have peace with you because of what your Son has done. And I confidently and joyfully look forward to sharing your glory. And I can rejoice, too, for problems and trials—they help me to develop strength. Thank you for giving me the Holy Spirit to fill my heart with your love. Now I know how dearly you love me.

Love Found a Way

Wonderful love that rescued me, sunk deep in sin,
Guilty and vile as I could be—no hope within;
When every ray of light had fled, O glorious day!
Raising my soul from out the dead, love found a way.

    Love found a way, to redeem my soul,
    Love found a way, that could make me whole.
    Love sent my Lord to the cross of shame,
    Love found a way, O praise his holy name!

Love brought my Savior here to die on Calvary,
For such a sinful wretch as I, how can it be?
Love bridged the gulf 'twixt me and heaven, taught me to pray,
I am redeemed, set free, forgiven, love found a way.

Love opened wide the gates of light to heaven's domain,
Where in eternal power and might Jesus shall reign.
Love lifted me from depths of woe to endless day,
There was no help in earth below, love found a way.

Avis Burgeson Christiansen (1895-1966)

Avis Burgeson began writing poetry as a child and became the author of hundreds of gospel hymns and two volumes of poetry. Born in Chicago, she married Ernest C. Christiansen, a longtime member of the staff of the Moody Bible Institute. Some of her first hymns were introduced by the choir of Moody Memorial Church where she was a member.

There was once a man who would unfurl a banner within the view of the cameras at nationally televised football games; on it was written *JOHN 3:16* in big, bold letters. No doubt some people wondered, "What is John 3:16?" And no doubt some discovered that it is a verse in the Bible that says, "For God so loved the world that he gave his only Son, so that everyone who believes in him may not perish but may have eternal life" (NRSV). We pray that many who saw the banner have believed its message and have found eternal life in Christ. Those who have, have found love.

The word *love* is bandied about in our culture like a Frisbee on a summer day. So much so that one of the poets of popular music concluded, "Love is just a four-letter word." This is indeed true, without the definition given in John 3:16: "God so loved the world that he gave . . ."

God is love—a well-known phrase among believers and non-believers alike. What is not so well known is that "God's love was revealed among us in this way: God sent his only Son into the world so that we might live through him" (1 John 4:9). This love, this sending of the Son, is called the *incarnation*—a wonderful term that indicates God's coming to us as a real man with flesh, blood, soul, everything but sin.

Today's hymn repeats, "Love found a way. Love found a way." Love's way is expressed by the gospel like this: "The Word became flesh and lived among us" (John 1:14). This is incarnation. This is real love. It is "not that we loved God but that he loved us and sent his Son to be the atoning sacrifice for our sins" (1 John 4:10).

RELATED SCRIPTURE READING—*1 John 5:11*

I worship you, my God. You are love; you found a way! You loved the world so much that you gave your only Son; now everyone who believes in him will have eternal life. Thank you for your wonderful way. I love your way of love!

Beneath the Cross of Jesus

Beneath the cross of Jesus I fain would take my stand,
The shadow of a mighty rock within a weary land.
A home within the wilderness, a rest upon the way,
From the burning of the noon-tide heat, and the burden of the day.

Upon the cross of Jesus mine eye at times can see
The very dying form of one who suffer'd there for me;
And from my smitten heart with tears two wonders I confess:
The wonders of redeeming love, and my own worthlessness.

I take, O cross, thy shadow for my abiding place;
I ask no other sunshine than the sunshine of his face;
Content to let the world go by, to know no gain nor loss,
My sinful self my only shame, my glory all the cross.

Elizabeth Cecilia Clephane (1830-1869)

This poet lived most of her short life in the former home of Sir Walter Scott near Abbotsford, Scotland. She earned the name "Sunbeam" from the poor and suffering of the community with whom she performed charitable work. She is best known for the hymns "Beneath the Cross of Jesus" and "The Ninety and Nine." Both were published posthumously, so she never heard them sung. It is said that the singer Ira Sankey found the words to "The Ninety and Nine" published in a newspaper as he traveled with D. L. Moody through Scotland and saved them in his pocket. Later when asked in a revival meeting to sing a hymn about the Good Shepherd, Sankey retrieved the words from his pocket, struck a chord, and composed the music to the hymn as he sang. This is the tune to which Clephane's hymn is sung today.

id you notice the two wonders mentioned in this hymn? The first is God's redeeming love. Christians celebrate this every week. What about the other wonder—your own worthlessness? Is this something to celebrate?

In a way we are *not* worthless. We may hold jobs and raise families, help others and contribute to the community, pass through suffering and generally live an upright life. These have value. But the Bible says, "For all have sinned; all fall short of God's glorious standard" (Romans 3:23 NLT).

The hymnist Elizabeth Clephane and the Bible itself do not speak of value and worthlessness as measured by human standards. Evaluate yourself by the divine standard—the glory of God. How do you rate? Worthless.

The shining of God's glory can be like the sun shining in Death Valley. There is no relief from its heat. Unless travelers find water and shelter, they will die. So God promised refreshment "as a river in the desert and as the cool shadow of a large rock in a hot and weary land" (Isaiah 32:2). But how does one find this river, this large rock?

Clephane reveals the secret: "I take, O cross, thy shadow for my abiding place." No matter how successful you may be by human standards, the world is still a human desert; true refreshment and lasting shelter can only be found in Christ. Each Sunday Christians celebrate the life, death, resurrection, ascension, and future coming of Jesus Christ. In the midst of this celebration of Christ's victory is our realization that we have failed to please God. We do not come up to God's glorious standard, but we have been given faith enough to hide in the forgiving shadow of the cross of Christ.

RELATED SCRIPTURE READING—*Psalm 55:4-8*

O Lord, sometimes my heart is in anguish and I am even afraid of death. Don't let these fears overwhelm me. I believe in you. Make me rest in the quiet of the wilderness, in the cooling shade and shelter of the redemption and forgiveness of your cross.

Lord, I Hear of Showers of Blessing

Lord, I hear of show'rs of blessing thou art scatt'ring full and free,
Show'rs the thirsty land refreshing; let some drops now fall on me.

Even me, even me,
Let some drops now fall on me.

Pass me not, O gracious Father! Sinful though my heart may be;
Thou might'st leave me, but the rather let thy mercy fall on me.

Pass me not, O tender Savior! Let me love and cling to thee;
I am longing for thy favor; while thou'rt calling, call for me.

Pass me not, O Lord, the Spirit! Thou canst make the blind to see;
By the witness of thy merit, speak the word of power to me.

Love of God, so pure and changeless! Blood of Christ, so rich and
free!
Grace of God, so strong and boundless! Magnify them all in me.

Pass me not! Thy lost one bringing, bind my heart, O Lord, to thee;
While the streams of life are springing, blessing others, O, bless me.

Elizabeth Harris Codner (1824-1919)

Married to the curate of Peterborough, England, Codner was editor of *Women's Work in the Great Harvest Field,* a monthly magazine published by the Mildmay Protestant Mission of North London. She published *The Missionary Ship, The Bible in the Kitchen,* and her hymns appeared in her book, *Among the Brambles and Other Lessons from Life.*

There was a man living in Jericho named Zacchaeus. Because he was a Roman tax collector he had become very rich and was one of the most influential Jews in the city. Once while Jesus passed through Jericho, Zacchaeus tried to get a look at him, but since he was too short to see over the crowd, he climbed a sycamore tree and watched from there.

When Jesus came along, he did not pass by; rather, he looked up at the man in the tree and called him by name. "Zacchaeus, hurry and come down; for I must stay at your house today" (Luke 19:5 NRSV). And so salvation came to the house of Zacchaeus.

Why did this happen? Jesus explained: "The Son of Man came to seek out and to save the lost" (v. 10). He was fulfilling a promise made centuries before to the leaders of Israel who had abandoned the people and were only caring for themselves. God said, "I myself will search for my sheep, and will seek them out" (Ezekiel 34:11). God also told them, "I will send down the showers in their season; they shall be showers of blessing" (v. 26).

What are these showers? Possessions? Position? Neither. Zacchaeus had all this and more. The showers of blessing began on earth when God came down in the person of Jesus Christ. Showers of blessing came to Zacchaeus and his family when Jesus arrived at their house.

Do you feel a little less than blessed? Look no further than Jesus Christ and pray, "Love of God, so pure and changeless! Blood of Christ, so rich and free! Grace of God, so strong and boundless! Magnify them all in me." He is God's blessing.

RELATED SCRIPTURE READING—*Ephesians 1:3*

Praise to you, God, for the wonderful kindness you have poured out on me because I belong to your dearly loved Son. You purchased my freedom through his blood, and my sins are forgiven. Thank you so much for this shower of kindness and wisdom and understanding.

O Christ, He Is the Fountain

O Christ, he is the fountain, the deep, sweet well of life:
Its living streams I've tasted which save from grief and strife.
And to an ocean fulness, his mercy doth expand;
His grace is all sufficient as by his wisdom planned.

O I am my Beloved's, and my beloved's mine;
He brings a poor vile sinner into his house of wine!
I stand upon his merit; I know no other stand.
I'm hidden in his presence and held by his own hand.

The Bride eyes not her garment, but her dear bridegroom's face;
I will not gaze at glory, but on my king of grace:
Not at the crown he giveth, but on his piercéd hand;
The Lamb is all the glory, and my eternal stand!

Anne Ross Cousin (1824–1906)

David Ross Cundell served as a surgeon at the Battle of Waterloo; Anne Ross was his daughter. Born at Hull, York, England, she grew up in the Church of England but later became a Presbyterian and married the Rev. William Cousin of the Scottish Free Church. Known as the "Scottish Christina Rossetti," her poems and hymns were published in *Immanuel's Land and Other Poems* (1876).

When you are riding in an airplane above the earth, are you flying? No, the airplane is flying and you are in the airplane. The plane is designed so it will overcome gravity; you are not.

This illustrates Anne Cousin's thought in the second verse of today's hymn: "I stand upon his merit" she says. "I know no other stand." Picture a stunt-flyer standing on the wing of a biplane as it flies above the countryside. Nothing but the aerodynamic merit of that airplane keeps him from falling to the fields below.

Just as you cannot fly unless you are in an airplane, so you cannot approach God unless you are in Christ. You cannot fly by running along flapping your arms, and you cannot please God by your own effort. Yet some people, figuratively speaking, spend all day flapping their arms—keeping rules, laws of behavior, and biblical principles—in the mistaken belief that this will make them acceptable to God (see Galatians 3:1–3). In fact, all they need do is believe the gospel and rest in Christ.

Certainly Christians are subject to the same suffering and difficulties that life can bring to all people. We are not flying above these things. But we are on a journey in Christ. Our destination is the New Jerusalem (see Revelation 21:1–4), and we are sure to arrive there where the Lamb is all the glory and our eternal stand!

The message of the gospel is like the boarding announcement in an airline terminal. Can you hear it inviting you into Christ? "The Spirit and the bride say, 'Come.' Let each one who hears them say, 'Come.' Let the thirsty ones come—anyone who wants to. Let them come and drink the water of life without charge" (Revelation 22:17 NLT).

RELATED SCRIPTURE READING—*Song of Songs 4:15-16*

Dear Father, your righteousness is like the mighty mountains, your justice like the ocean depths. How precious is your unfailing love, O God! You feed me from the abundance of your own house, letting me drink from your rivers of delight. You are the fountain of life, the light by which I see.

Sing Praise to God Who Reigns Above

Sing praise to God who reigns above, the God of all creation,
The God of power, the God of love, the God of our salvation;
With healing balm my soul he fills, and every faithless murmur stills:
    To God all praise and glory.

What God's almighty power hath made, his gracious mercy keepeth;
By morning flow or evening shade his watchful eye ne'er sleepeth.
Within the kingdom of his might, lo! all is just and all is right:
    To God all praise and glory.

Let all who name Christ's holy name give God all praise and glory;
Let all who know his power proclaim aloud the wondrous story!
Cast each false idol from its throne, the Lord is God, and he alone:
    To God all praise and glory.

Frances Elizabeth Cox (1812-1897)—Translator

Frances Cox is remembered for her translation of German hymns into English, and her work was included in the hymnal *Sacred Hymns from the German* (1841). In the second edition, *Hymns from the German,* her original forty-nine translations were modified and enlarged with twenty newly translated hymns.

e English-speaking Christians must, of all peoples, remember our debt to other languages, cultures, and nations. Without the Jewish nation we would not have a Savior—Jesus was a Jew. Not only so, without their faithfulness we would not have the Old Testament, which forms the foundation of the New. There is no space here to review the church's history as it moved from Jerusalem through today's Syria and Turkey to Greece, Italy, the European continent, and the British Isles.

There, England experienced the convulsions of church reformation in the sixteenth century; but the world was truly shaken by the reformation on the Continent. The church, politics, economics, language, civic life, the arts, and much more were revolutionized by the German Martin Luther and the French John Calvin. If the church is spiritually rich today, it is only because we can draw interest off the investments of these and many other believers.

Today's hymn of praise to God was written in German by Johann Jacob Schütz (1640–1690) and translated into English by Frances Elizabeth Cox (1812–1897). Thanks to the faithful work of Ms. Cox, Americans can express love to God with these beautiful words.

The author and the translator of this hymn lived two hundred years apart, one in Germany, the other in England; one was male, the other female, one Lutheran, the other Anglican. This is glory to God, because it fulfills the vision of Scripture for the church where "there is no longer Jew or Gentile, slave or free, male or female. For you are all Christians—you are one in Christ Jesus" (Galatians 3:28 NLT).

RELATED SCRIPTURE READING—*1 Corinthians 12:13*

Father God, hear my prayer for the church. Truly make it a place where the differences of culture and religion are dissolved. Banish the love of money from your house of prayer. And, O Lord, let there be no battle of the sexes in your family. Remind us again and again that we are one in Christ Jesus.

God Rest Ye Merry, Gentlemen

God rest ye merry, gentlemen, let nothing you dismay;
Remember Christ our Savior was born on Christmas Day,
To save us all from Satan's power when we were gone astray.

    O tidings of comfort and joy, comfort and joy;
    O tidings of comfort and joy.

From God our heavenly Father a blessed angel came
And unto certain shepherds brought tidings of the same:
How that in Bethlehem was born the Son of God by name.

"Fear not, then," said the angel, "let nothing you affright;
This day is born a Savior of a pure virgin bright,
To free all those who trust in him from Satan's power and might."

Now to the Lord sing praises, all you within this place,
And with true love and charity each other now embrace;
This holy tide of Christmas doth bring redeeming grace.

Dinah Maria Craik (1826-1887)

Born in Staffordshire, England, Dinah Maria Mulock went to London about 1846 and wrote *The Ogilvies* (1849) and many other books and short stories. There she married George L. Craik of the publishing house of Macmillan and Company. Her hymn appeared in *Golden Numbers* (1902) and is a variation of a carol by an unknown hymnist.

When I hear this old English carol I see a street scene on a crisp, wintry evening in London town. Large flakes of snow are falling and sticking to men's tall hats as they hurry here and there—merry gentlemen one and all. The lamplighter is making his rounds and joy fills the air. It is Christmas Eve, and—oh! did I just see Bob Cratchit go by carrying Tiny Tim?

You see what I mean? The song summons the secular sentiments attached to the holiday. St. Nicholas and all that. And, if not taken too seriously, there is nothing so wrong with these sentiments. I find pleasure in the pretty lights that appear as the winter nights grow long, don't you? I like to consider my loved ones as I purchase a gift and remember old friends as I open a card.

Much about the Christmas season is pleasant. Especially if you are careful not to allow the waves of commercialism and acquisition to knock you off your feet. And, for many people it is the only time they attend a church service. There they may hear the tidings that certain shepherds once heard: "How that in Bethlehem was born the Son of God by name."

So now is the time to begin to pray for these people who do not yet know the tidings of comfort and joy that are brought by this and so many other Christmas hymns. Ask the Lord that the day will come when they know the joy in the words, "Now to the Lord sing praises, all you within this place, / And with true love and charity each other now embrace." Let them be caught in a holy tide at Christmas that brings redeeming grace.

RELATED SCRIPTURE READING—*Luke 2:8-14*

O Savior, Jesus Christ, millions of people have not yet truly heard these tidings of comfort and joy—you came to live and die among us. Cut through the potent attractions and distractions of the secular seasons and let our loved ones and neighbors hear in their hearts the angel's words: "This day is born a Savior of a pure virgin bright, to free all those who trust in him from Satan's power and might."

Praise Him! Praise Him!

Praise him! praise him! Jesus, our blessed redeemer!
　　Sing, ye saints! his wonderful love proclaim!
Hail him! hail him! mightiest angels in glory;
　　Strength and honor give to his holy name!
Like a shepherd, Jesus will feed his people,
　　In his arms He carries them all day long;
O ye saints that live in the light of his presence,
　　Praise him! praise him! ever in joyful song!

Praise him! praise him! Jesus, our blessed redeemer,
　　For our sins he suffered and bled and died;
He, our rock, our hope of eternal salvation,
　　Hail him! hail him! Jesus, the crucified;
Loving Savior, meekly enduring sorrow,
　　Crowned with thorns that cruelly pierced his brow;
Once for us rejected, despised, and forsaken,
　　Prince of glory, ever triumphant now.

Fanny Crosby (1820-1915)

Frances Jane Crosby was born in Putnam County, New York. She lost her eyesight at six weeks of age and was blind for the remainder of her life. Crosby was educated at the New York Institute for the Blind and was a student of composer George F. Root. She wrote lyrics for some of his popular songs. The number of hymns and poems Crosby wrote has been variously reported—anywhere between four and eight thousand. Her hymns are found in nearly every modern American hymnal.

This triumphant song could be sung for the processional entrance of the greatest of kings. But what kind of king is this who does not wear a kingly crown? Fanny Crosby points out that Jesus Christ's crown is made of thorns; the very thorns we cut and scrape from the earth. We chop, burn, or dump them to rid them from our lives. They are the weeds, brambles, and choking vines that return to our land year after year from the earth's waste places; the tumbleweeds driven by endless dry winds that line our fences like spectators to the vanity of our effort to eradicate them.

There was no need to dig deep in the earth to extract the materials for Christ's crown. His diadem is found lying on the surface of every human life. No refining, cutting, polishing; no fine work of an artisan is needed. Since the night a rude Roman soldier laughingly crafted this crown, anyone can plait together the thorny weeds of their life to decorate the brow of Jesus.

"I have placed a curse on the ground, . . ." God told the man. "It will grow thorns and thistles for you, . . ." (Genesis 3:17–18 NLT). Today we still live under this curse. Yet our curse became Christ's crown. The Bible explains: "When he was hung on the cross, he took upon himself the curse for our wrongdoing. . . . Through the work of Christ Jesus, God has blessed the Gentiles with the same blessing he promised to Abraham, and we Christians receive the promised Holy Spirit through faith" (Galatians 3:13–14).

So each of us actually has a crown to place on the Savior's head. We weave the crowns from the thorns of our own life and he makes them holy. This gives new meaning to the words of Matthew Bridges's hymn "Crown Him with Many Crowns."

RELATED SCRIPTURE READING—*Matthew 26:39*

Lord Jesus Christ, I love you. Thank you for wearing a crown for me—the bloody crown of my sinfulness. Thank you that you drank deeply from the cup of God's curse so that humanity can drink from the cup of God's blessing. Let me taste again the freshness of that cup and help me remember the millions who have not yet tasted the blessings of your redemption.

Whom Have I in Heav'n Above?

Whom have I in heav'n above? Only thee, my Savior;
Whom have I on earth to love? Only thee, my Savior;
Who my wounded heart can heal, who my every sorrow feel,
Who the light of joy reveal? Only thee, my Savior.

Who has led me all my days? Only thou, my Savior;
Who deserves my highest praise? Only thou, my Savior;
In my weakness who is strong, who has loved and loved me long,
Who should claim my noblest song? Only thou, my Savior.

Who my inmost thoughts can read? Only thou, my Savior;
Who for me doth intercede? Only thou, my Savior;
Who my secret thoughts can know, who such tender mercy show,
Who can make me white as snow? Only thou, my Savior.

Fanny Crosby (1820–1915)

anny Crosby's songs are wonderfully modest. And though her songs are simple, her questions are not.

Whom do you have on earth? What relationship in this life is absolutely dependable, lasting to the end? Don't let these questions sadden you. Yes, we have loved ones and friends. The things of this life do have their value and their place. But in the end, all a Christian truly owns is Christ.

The psalmist Asaph wrote: "Whom have I in heaven but you? I desire you more than anything on earth. My health may fail, and my spirit may grow weak, but God remains the strength of my heart; he is mine forever" (Psalm 73:25–26 NLT).

Are there some things on earth that you desire more than God? This was true of the psalmist Asaph too. He was envious of the ambitious and successful people around him (73:3); he thought they were healthy and free of life's difficulties (vv. 4–5); he saw how people admired them (v. 10). He had the notion they were simply enjoying a life of ease while their riches multiplied (v. 12). He wanted to be like them.

Asaph was embittered by this. But then he saw that his perceptions of the world around him were stupid. "I realized how bitter I had become, how pained I had been by all I had seen," he wrote. "I was so foolish and ignorant—I must have seemed like a senseless animal to you. Yet I still belong to you; you are holding my right hand. You will keep on guiding me with your counsel, leading me to a glorious destiny" (vv. 21–24).

Let's ask Asaph, "How did you find this understanding and peace?" His answer: "One day I went into God's sanctuary" (see Psalm 73:17). This is the never-failing balm for a troubled heart.

RELATED SCRIPTURE READING—*Philippians 4:6-7*

Lord, you know that there is trouble in my life and among those I love. Don't let me be discouraged by these things. Instead, I bring them to you in prayer. I will never find a friend so faithful as you who will share all of my sorrows. You know every one of my weaknesses; I bring them to you in the sanctuary of prayer.

47

My Faith Has Found a Resting Place

My faith has found a resting place, not in device nor creed;
I trust the ever-living one, his wounds for me shall plead.

I need no other argument, I need no other plea;
It is enough that Jesus died, and that he died for me.

Enough for me that Jesus saves, this ends my fear and doubt;
A sinful soul I come to him, he'll never cast me out.

My heart is leaning on the Word, the written Word of God,
Salvation by my Savior's name, salvation through his blood.

My great Physician heals the sick, the lost he came to save;
For me his precious blood he shed, for me his life he gave.

Lidie H. Edmunds (1849-1889)

Lidie H. Edmunds lived in Bristol, England, and there enjoyed fellowship with the Plymouth Brethren. Her hymn was published in 1891 in *Hymns of Joy and Gladness, No. 2.*

God's purpose abides upon layers of rest. God rested after the creation. The fourth commandment was given with the intent that Israel might rest as well (Exodus 20:8–11). Moreover the land of Israel was to be worked for six years "but in the seventh year there [was to be] a sabbath of complete rest for the land" (Leviticus 25:4 NRSV). However, there is no record that this Sabbath was observed. The land did not enjoy its rest for the nearly five hundred years of Israel's inhabitation. So God intervened, Israel was taken away captive for seventy years, and the land enjoyed its promised rest. Rest is important to God.

Eventually the Jews were reestablished in the land. But they firmly yoked themselves to the law. God did not intend anyone should carry this heavy load. So Jesus Christ appeared saying, "Come unto me, all you that are weary and are carrying heavy burdens, and I will give you rest. Take my yoke upon you, . . . and you will find rest for your souls" (Matthew 11:28–29). This is why Lidie Edmunds writes, "My faith has found a resting place."

God finished the work of creation then rested. The Jewish Sabbath commemorates this rest. Then God set out on another task—"the Son of Man came to seek out and to save the lost" (Luke 19:10). This tremendous quest led Jesus to the cross where he at last said "It is finished" and died—full redemption was accomplished (John 19:30). None of us could have done this work; nor is there a need for God to do it again—both we and God can rest.

RELATED SCRIPTURE READING—*Galatians 2:19-20*

Dear God, save me from attempting to find a resting place for my faith in any method, creed, or group. Instead, strengthen my trust in your Son, the ever-living one. His wounds plead for me. Father, I hear of many arguments on this earth, even among Christians. But I need no other argument; it is enough that your Son died for me.

Just As I Am

Just as I am, without one plea,
But that thy blood was shed for me,
And that Thou bidd'st me come to Thee,
O Lamb of God, I come, I come!

Just as I am, and waiting not
To rid my soul of one dark blot;
To Thee whose blood can cleanse each spot,
O Lamb of God, I come, I come!

Just as I am, though tossed about
With many a conflict, many a doubt;
Fightings within, and fears without,
O Lamb of God, I come, I come!

Just as I am, poor, wretched, blind;
Sight, riches, healing of the mind;
Yes, all I need, in thee to find,
O Lamb of God, I come, I come!

Just as I am, thou wilt receive,
Wilt welcome, pardon, cleanse, relieve;
Because thy promise I believe,
O Lamb of God, I come, I come!

Just as I am, thy love unknown
Has broken every barrier down;
Now, to be thine, yea, thine alone,
O Lamb of God, I come, I come!

Charlotte Elliott (1789-1871)

A Swiss evangelist named Caesar Malan once visited the family home of Charlotte Elliott in London. He expressed the truth of the gospel to Ms. Elliott in such a way that she not only believed in Jesus but wrote one of the most popular of the church's gospel hymns ("Just As I Am"). Thereafter Elliott and Malan corresponded for forty years. Elliott was editor of the annual *Christian Remembrancer Pocketbook* for twenty-five years and assisted in the publication of the *Invalid's Hymn Book,* which contained 112 of her poems. She wrote 150 hymns that address the concerns of those in sickness and sorrow.

Jesus told the story of two men who went up to the temple to pray. One was a Pharisee and the other a tax collector. "The Pharisee stood up and prayed about himself: 'God, I thank you that I am not like other men—robbers, evildoers, adulterers—or even like this tax collector. I fast twice a week and give a tenth of all I get.' But the tax collector stood at a distance. He would not even look up to heaven, but beat his breast and said, 'God, have mercy on me, a sinner'" (Luke 18:11–13 NIV).

Here is Jesus' lesson in this story: "I tell you that this [tax collector], rather than the other, went home justified before God" (Luke 18:14).

One man was humble, the other self-exalting. What was the Pharisee so exultant about? His goodness. Why was the tax collector so humble? He knew he was a sinner. In fact, they were both sinners, but only one admitted to this.

We do not have to be on our best behavior to come to God. Our best is not good enough. As Jesus said, "No one is good—except God alone" (Mark 10:18). God is not like Santa Claus who, as the tale says, keeps a list of the naughty and nice. There is no need of a list since "all have sinned and fall short of the glory of God" (Romans 3:23).

No amount of self-improvement can bring you to the level of God. For this reason, everyone must sing, "Just as I am, without one plea, but that thy blood was shed for me, and that thou bidd'st me come to thee, O Lamb of God, I come, I come!"

RELATED SCRIPTURE READING—*Acts 17:26-28*

Lord, I want to be a good person, treat others right, and make a difference in my family and maybe even in this world. But I ask you to save me from being haughty. Help me to understand that all the nations on earth come from the same source. You decide who will rise and fall. You determine our boundaries. So Lord, I ask that you will cause the nations to seek you, feel their way toward you, and find you.

Jesus, My Savior, Look on Me

Jesus my Savior, look on me, for I am weary and oppressed;
I come to cast myself on thee: Thou art my rest.

Look down on me, for I am weak; I feel the toilsome journey's length:
Thine aid omnipotent I seek: Thou art my strength.

I am bewilder'd on my way, dark and tempestuous is the night;
O send thou forth some cheering ray! Thou art my light.

When Satan flings his fiery darts, I look to thee; my terrors cease;
Thy cross a hiding place imparts: Thou art my peace.

Standing alone on Jordan's brink, in that tremendous, latest strife,
Thou wilt not suffer me to sink: Thou art my life.

Thou wilt my every want supply, e'en to the end, whate'er befall:
Through life, in death, eternally, Thou art my all.

Charlotte Elliott (1789–1871)

Charlotte Elliott is best known for writing "Just As I Am without One Plea," a gospel hymn that has helped many people begin their life of faith in Jesus Christ. From today's hymn we see that Elliott not only learned the secret of beginning the Christian life by faith, she also knew how to continue in faith.

In beginning her life of faith Elliott came to God just as she was, "waiting not to rid my soul of one dark blot." She had found that nothing she could do would erase those blots. And so she sang, "To thee whose blood can cleanse each spot, O Lamb of God, I come."

Imagine a conversation between the apostle Paul and Charlotte Elliott: "Did you receive the Holy Spirit by keeping the law?" asks the apostle. Elliott replies, "Of course not." He responds, "[Right!] For the Holy Spirit came upon you only after you believed the message you heard about Christ" (Galatians 3:2 NLT).

After this wonderful experience of believing the gospel, too many people try to live the Christian life by keeping rules and applying biblical principles. To this Paul says, "Have you lost your senses? After starting your Christian lives in the Spirit, why are you now trying to become perfect by your own human effort?" (v. 3). This brings us to today's hymn.

Charlotte Elliott says to Christ, "Thou art my rest, my strength, my light, my peace, my life, and my all." She understood that in this Christian life, it doesn't matter who you are or what you can do. "Christ is all that matters, and he lives in [and for] all of us" (Colossians 3:11).

RELATED SCRIPTURE READING—*Ephesians 3:8*

Lord, when I look for rest or strength or light from some other source besides you, remind me of the boundless riches of Christ. When the pleasures of the earth wane and I am dissatisfied even with myself, remind me of the beloved Son in whom you are well pleased and teach me to sing, "Thou art my peace. Thou art my life. Thou art my all."

I Love My Lord, But with No Love of Mine

I love my Lord, but with no love of mine,
    For I have none to give;
I love thee, Lord, but all the love is thine,
    For by thy love I live.
I am as nothing, and rejoice to be
    Emptied, and lost,
        and swallow'd up in thee.

Thou, Lord, alone, art all thy children need,
    And there is none beside;
From thee the streams of blessedness proceed,
    In thee the bless'd abide.
Fountain of life, and all-abounding grace,
    Our source, our center,
        and our dwelling-place.

Madame Jeanne Guyon (1648–1717)

This French aristocrat and mystic was educated in convents and, as a child, was drawn to the religious life. But she was forced to marry at age fifteen. In the midst of this miserable marriage she resorted to prayer and, according to her autobiography, after four years as a widow, she had a religious experience of mystical union with God. This brought her both disciples and enemies. Although Madame Guyon became influential at the French court, she was eventually suppressed by the church and confined for a time in a convent and later in the Bastille. Finally she was officially censured and so lived out her life quietly in Blois, France. Thirty-seven of her poems and hymns were translated by the English poet William Cowper and published in 1801.

ove the Lord your God with all your heart and with all your soul and with all your mind.' This is the first and greatest commandment" (Matthew 22:37–38 NIV). In this mystical hymn, Madame Guyon helps us understand how it is possible to fulfill the greatest commandment. "I love thee, Lord," she says, "but all the love is thine."

Let's piece together this puzzle of love from the Scripture. We know that "whoever does not love does not know God, because God is love" (1 John 4:8). Yet how can we know God? Thankfully God loved us first by sending the Son to make the Father known (see 1 John 4:10). Believers love God because Jesus Christ lived his earthly life expressing the Father and died his redeeming death to bring us to God.

Love has its source in God who sent the Son. God's love in the Son enters our hearts when we believe and returns to God in our prayer and worship. Why do we love God? Because we know and believe the birth and life, death and resurrection of Jesus Christ, the Son of God.

Yes! It is possible to love God in the way the greatest commandment describes. Just as water fills one cell of an ice tray and flows over into the next, so God's love in Christ overflows from the Holy Spirit into our heart and then into our understanding through the Word of God. As this process continues we joy to pray, "I love you, Lord, but all the love is yours."

RELATED SCRIPTURE READING—*Deuteronomy 6:4-6*

Father, I pray for my friends in the faith. May we love one another with the love that comes from you. May we love you like children who are born of you and know you. And I pray for people who do not know you and so must struggle to love. Bring them to the lifesaving knowledge that you are love.

Tell Me the Old, Old Story

Tell me the old, old story of unseen things above,
Of Jesus and his glory, of Jesus and his love.
Tell me the story simply, as to a little child;
For I am weak and weary, and helpless and defiled.

> Tell me the old, old story,
> Tell me the old, old story,
> Tell me the old, old story
> Of Jesus and his love.

Tell me the story slowly, that I may take it in—
That wonderful redemption, God's remedy for sin.
Tell me the story often, for I forget so soon;
The early dew of morning has passed away at noon.

Tell me the same old story when you have cause to fear
That this world's empty glory is costing me too dear.
Yes, and when that world's glory is dawning on my soul,
Tell me the old, old story: "Christ Jesus makes thee whole."

Katherine Hankey (1834-1911)

At age eighteen Kate Hankey began to teach Sunday school classes for people of her own social circle (her father was an English banker) and for London's working women. In 1866 she wrote a book in verse about the life of Jesus titled *The Old, Old Story*. Part One of this poem, "The Story Wanted," includes the words to Hankey's hymn "I Love to Tell the Story." Her hymn "Tell Me the Old, Old Story" comes from Part Two of the book, "The Story Told." Part Three is titled "The Story Welcomed." These hymns were first published in *Music for Camp Meetings* (1872).

*R*eading these lyrics it seems that it was quite crucial that Katherine Hankey hear the story of Jesus and his love. What caused her to know her weak, helpless state? We don't really know, and we don't really need to know. Each of us has our own life and each needs help in living it.

A large portion of nonfiction book publishing today is devoted to a category called *Self-Help*. Some self-help books are so popular that they remain on best-seller lists for months, even years. Publishers issue new titles every year. This not only means that publishers hope to profit from the self-help industry but also that people know they need help living their lives. They want advice, counsel, stories, wisdom, hope. This is true of both Christians and non-Christians.

Katherine Hankey lived in England in the late nineteenth century. There was no self-help industry to speak of at that time. But she needed help just as you and I do today. What causes you to realize that *you* are weak, weary, helpless, or defiled? Your job, marriage, children? The television, your finances, the world situation? Change comes so very slowly. In the meantime you need advice, counsel, stories, wisdom, hope. Please, don't look elsewhere for these. Return to the Bible—the old, old story of Jesus and his love.

Pick up the book and read it in faith. "The LORD is my shepherd; I have everything I need. . . . Even when I walk through the dark valley of death, I will not be afraid, for you are close beside me. . . . Surely your goodness and unfailing love will pursue me all the days of my life, and I will live in the house of the LORD forever" (Psalm 23:1, 4, 6 NLT).

RELATED SCRIPTURE READING—*Luke 24:27*

Dear Lord Jesus Christ, Son of God, Word of God, the next time I read the Bible, tell me the old, old story. Interpret to me the things about yourself in the Scriptures. "Tell me the story simply, as to a little child; for I am weak and weary, and helpless and defiled."

Like a River, Glorious

Like a river, glorious
　　Is God's perfect peace,
Over all victorious
　　In its bright increase,
Perfect, yet it floweth
　　Fuller ev'ry day,
Perfect, yet it groweth
　　Deeper all the way.

　Stayed upon Christ Jesus,
　Hearts are fully blest;
　Finding, as he promised,
　Perfect peace and rest.

Hidden in the hollow
　　Of his blessed hand,
Never foe can follow,
　　Never traitor stand;
Not a surge of worry,
　　Not a shade of care,
Not a blast of hurry
　　Touch the spirit there.

Every joy or trial
　　Falleth from above,
Traced upon our dial
　　By the Sun of Love
We may trust him fully
　　All for us to do;
They who trust him wholly
　　Find him wholly true.

Frances R. Havergal (1836-1879)

Born in Worcestershire, England, Frances Havergal was educated there and in Düsseldorf, Germany. She wrote many hymns that emphasize faith, devotion, and service to God. "Take My Life and Let It Be" is among them.

Other hymns by Frances Havergal include "Who Is on the Lord's Side?", "Thou Art Coming, O My Savior," and "I Am Trusting Thee, Lord Jesus." A volume of her poetry titled *Poetical Works* was published in 1884. Her prose writings include *Kept for the Master's Use* and *Royal Commandments and Royal Bounty*.

Every river has its source in some secret place far away. The Connecticut River begins its 450-mile course to Long Island Sound by quietly trickling through an old beaver dam within hailing distance of Canada. Northwest of Brainerd, Minnesota, is a stream deep in the woods. There, with a small leap, you can easily cross the Mississippi River, because this is the great river's headwater. The river of God's peace has headwaters as well. To enjoy this river, journey to its source.

Peace begins in God. This is true. But it is also true that the Mississippi begins in the rain clouds. These are not readily accessible to us. We need God's peace flowing in us daily, even hourly. God is not far away from us; our spiritual peace springs from a very practical source.

As always, the Bible points the way. "Unfailing love and truth have met together" sings the psalmist. "Righteousness and peace have kissed!" (Psalm 85:10 NLT). When and where did this sweet embrace occur? During the violence at the cross of Jesus Christ. There "God made him who had no sin to be sin for us, so that in him we might become the righteousness of God" (2 Corinthians 5:21 NIV). This is the righteousness that kisses peace.

When you find this righteousness you are wading in the headwaters of the river of peace. The gospel reveals "a righteousness that is by faith from first to last" (Romans 1:17). How do we find peace? Through this righteousness. Does this mean we must behave in a certain way? No. "This righteousness from God comes through faith in Jesus Christ" (Romans 3:22). Have faith in Christ; find peace.

RELATED SCRIPTURE READING—*Romans 5:1-2*

O righteous God, thank you that I have been made right in your sight by faith. I have peace with you because of what Jesus Christ my Lord has done for me. And thank you that Christ has brought me into a place of highest privilege where I now stand; I joyfully look forward to sharing your glory.

Take My Life, and Let It Be

Take my life, and let it be consecrated, Lord, to thee.
Take my moments and my days; let them flow in ceaseless praise.
Take my hands, and let them move at the impulse of thy love.
Take my feet, and let them be swift and beautiful for thee.

Take my voice, and let me sing always, only, for my king.
Take my lips, and let them be filled with messages from thee.
Take my silver and my gold; not a mite would I withhold.
Take my intellect, and use every power as Thou shalt choose.

Take my will, and make it thine; it shall be no longer mine.
Take my heart, it is thine own; it shall be thy royal throne.
Take my love, my Lord, I pour at thy feet its treasure store.
Take myself, and I will be ever, only, all for thee.

Frances R. Havergal (1836–1879)

When the apostle Paul was still called Saul, he approved the death of Stephen (Acts 8:1), breathed murderous threats (9:1), had a reputation for evil, made havoc with the church, and persecuted it to death (vv. 13, 21; 22:4, 19). Later Paul ruefully confessed, "I am not worthy to be called an apostle after the way I persecuted the church of God" (1 Corinthians 15:9 NLT).

Nonetheless Paul is arguably the most significant of all God's servants. What happened? Did he decide to change? Hardly. His oppression of the church continued unabated. But while he was on his way to Damascus to arrest believers there he was blinded by a bright light and, falling to the ground, heard a voice: "I am Jesus of Nazareth, the one you are persecuting" (Acts 22:8).

In today's hymn, Frances Havergal sings, "Take my life, and let it be consecrated, Lord, to thee." The word *consecrated* means *devoted entirely, dedicated*. Havergal goes on to list everything she desires the Lord to take—moments and days, hands and feet, voice and lips, silver and gold, intellect and will, heart and love— a very complete list. Its sum: her entire self.

The notable word in this hymn is *take*. Havergal is submitting herself to God. She is simply making herself available for the divine purpose. She is not insisting; she is not trying to improve; she is not presumptuous.

Saul had no intention of being consecrated to the service of the church of God. He was dedicated to destroying it. But God took him. No one can demand to be used by God. This is useless. The best we can do is be available to God, praying, "Take me."

RELATED SCRIPTURE READING—*Luke 7:36-38*

Lord, take my will; make it yours, and it will not be mine anymore. Take my heart; it is yours. Make it into your throne. Take my love, Lord; it is my only treasure. I pour it at your feet. And I pray that one day you will take my entire self. Then I will be ever, only, and all for you.

Another Year Is Dawning

Another year is dawning, dear Father, let it be
In working or in waiting, another year with thee.
Another year of progress, another year of praise,
Another year of proving thy presence all the days.

Another year of mercies, of faithfulness and grace,
Another year of gladness in the shining of thy face;
Another year of leaning upon thy loving breast;
Another year of trusting, of quiet, happy rest.

Another year of service, of witness for thy love,
Another year of training for holier work above.
Another year is dawning, dear Father, let it be
On earth, or else in heaven, another year for thee.

Frances R. Havergal (1836-1879)

Frances Havergal was the master of several languages, including Latin, Hebrew, Greek, French, and German. She was a natural musician with a pleasing, well-trained voice and a brilliant hand at the piano. And although she died 120 years ago, her hymns are loved and sung still today.

We live in a world of tedious jobs, stress at home, and financial pressure, with no relief in sight. On some days, to sing "Another year of progress, another year of praise, / Another year of proving thy presence all the days," would seem ludicrous. Actually it is the difficult days that are the best for hymn-singing. They are excellent for proving God's presence.

Remember, no one is exempt from the difficulties of human life. One of Frances Havergal's best-loved hymns is "I Gave My Life for Thee," written when she was only eighteen. But thereafter she suffered an extended illness and did little or no writing for nine years. She lived to be forty-three years old, so her adulthood lasted only twenty-five years. Nine of these years were spent in illness—no hymns were written. This means she had about fourteen productive years.

It is fruitless to idealize someone else's life or to expect that our own life will be without difficulties. Instead we can give our days to God—even our tedious, trivial days—by singing, "Another year of mercies, of faithfulness and grace, / Another year of gladness in the shining of thy face; / Another year of leaning upon thy loving breast; / Another year of trusting, of quiet, happy rest."

RELATED SCRIPTURE READING—*Luke 8:1-3*

Dear God, when I look up at the night sky and see your handiwork—the moon and the stars you have set in place—what are human beings that you should even think of us? Why should you care for us? But I know that you do. So dear Father, here I have another day. Let it be, in working or in waiting, another day with you.

Fear Not, I Am with Thee

"Fear not, I am with thee"; blessed golden ray,
Like a star of glory, lighting up my way!
Through the clouds of midnight, this bright promise shone,
"I will never leave thee, never will leave thee alone."

No, never alone, no, never alone;
He promised never to leave me,
Never to leave me alone.

Roses fade around me, lilies bloom and die,
Earthly sunbeams vanish—radiant still the sky!
Jesus, fairest flower, blooming for his own,
Jesus, heaven's sunshine, never will leave me alone.

Steps unseen before me, hidden dangers near:
Nearer still my Savior, whispering, "Be of cheer";
Joys, like birds of springtime, to my heart have flown,
Singing all so sweetly, "He will not leave me alone."

Eliza Hewitt (1851-1920)

Hewitt graduated valedictorian of her class at Philadelphia's Girls Normal School and taught in public schools. She was superintendent of the Sunday school of the Northern Home for Friendless Children and later of the Calvin Presbyterian Church in Philadelphia. Other favorite hymns by Eliza Hewitt are: "More about Jesus Would I Know," "Sing the Wondrous Love of Jesus," and "There Is Sunshine in My Soul Today."

Jesus once told his disciples, "Dear children, how brief are these moments before I must go away and leave you! Then, though you search for me, you cannot come to me" (John 13:33 NLT). Naturally, this disturbed the disciples. So Jesus tried to reassure them: "Don't be troubled. You trust God, now trust in me" (John 14:1). They knew that "he would suffer. . . . He would be killed, and he would be raised on the third day" (Matthew 16:21). He wanted them to trust that he would be resurrected. Though Jesus said, "you cannot come to me," he went on to say, "I will not abandon you as orphans— *I will come to you*" (John 14:18, italics added).

And the Lord did come to them—and to us—in resurrection. This is why the warm words of today's hymn are so comforting. "He promised never to leave me alone."

Jesus did not speak the words "I will come to you" only as a man. He was speaking as God. Father, Son, and Spirit are, mysteriously, one God. Just before Jesus ascended into heaven he promised his disciples that the Holy Spirit would come upon them (Acts 1:8). This indeed happened on the day of Pentecost (2:4). The believers were not left alone like orphans—God had come to them as the Spirit just as God had come to humanity thirty-three years before as the Son!

The disciples were sorrowful when Christ was betrayed and crucified. But he fulfilled his word: "I will see you again; then you will rejoice, and no one can rob you of that joy" (John 16:22). So we can sing with Eliza Hewitt, "Joys, like birds of springtime, to my heart have flown, singing all so sweetly, 'He will not leave me alone.'"

RELATED SCRIPTURE READING—*Mark 14:50*

Lord, I know that you were nailed to a cross. You were alone, dying, separated from everyone and everything, including God; all so that I would not be alone in this world or in eternity. I renew my faith in you, Lord Jesus. Thank you for all you have done.

On This Day Earth Shall Ring

On this day earth shall ring with the song children sing
    To the Lord, Christ our King,
Born on earth to save us; him the Father gave us.

Ideo gloria in excelsis Deo! [Therefore, glory to God in the highest]

His the doom, ours the mirth; when he came down to earth
    Bethlehem saw his birth.
Ox and ass beside him from the cold would hide him.

God's bright star, o'er his head, Wise Men three to him led;
    Kneel they low by his bed,
Lay their gifts before him, praise him and adore him.

On this day angels sing; with their song earth shall ring,
    Praising Christ, heaven's king,
Born on earth to save us; peace and love he gave us.

Jane M. Joseph (1894-1921)—Translator

This hymn is Jane Joseph's translation from the Swedish. She was a gifted English musician who studied under Gustav Holst, the British composer of *The Planets Suite, The Hymn of Jesus,* and the music for Christina Rossetti's hymn "In the Bleak Midwinter" (see page 88).

During the first weekend of July, West Jefferson, in Ashe County, North Carolina, holds a "Christmas in July" festival. The streets are lined with decorated evergreen trees and strung with lights while people enjoy a three-day street fair and bazaar. Ashe County is home to Christmas tree farms and claims the title "Christmas Tree Capital of the World." So while the rest of the country is observing the Fourth of July, Ashe County celebrates Christmas.

Many of the secular customs now associated with Christmas—decorating with holly and ivy, excessive eating and drinking, and exchanging gifts—can be traced back to early pagan festivals. Even the Christmas tree originates in ancient times when trees were worshipped as spirits.

For Christians, Christmas represents much more. It commemorates the incarnation of God—the birth of Jesus, the Savior. But it has become difficult if not impossible to separate the secular from the sacred during the December holiday season, even for the most observant Christian. In fact, the holy has been choked by the profane.

Which brings us back to Christmas in July. Here's an idea: Why not celebrate incarnation every day? An ancient hymn is quoted in Philippians: "Though he was God, . . . He made himself nothing; he took the humble position of a slave and appeared in human form. And in human form he obediently humbled himself even further by dying a criminal's death on a cross. Because of this, God raised him up to the heights of heaven and gave him a name that is above every other name" (2:6–9 NLT).

The recollection of this marvelous act of God marks the Christian soul and guides our faith every day.

RELATED SCRIPTURE READING—*Isaiah 9:6*

O heavenly Father, I believe that Mary conceived and bore a son and named him Jesus. And the child was holy and called Son of God. Nothing is impossible with you. I believe that you, O God, were born as the child Jesus, the Savior you have given to all people. He is a light to reveal you to the nations, and he is the glory of your people Israel!

Break Thou the Bread of Life

Break thou the bread of life, dear Lord, to me,
As thou didst break the loaves beside the sea;
Beyond the sacred page I seek thee, Lord;
My spirit pants for thee, O living Word.

Thou art the bread of life, O Lord, to me,
Thy holy Word the truth that saveth me;
Give me to eat and live with thee above;
Teach me to love thy truth, for thou art love.

Oh, send thy Spirit, Lord, now unto me,
That he may touch my eyes, and make me see;
Show me the truth concealed within thy word,
And in thy book revealed I see the Lord.

Bless thou the truth, dear Lord, to me, to me,
As thou didst bless the bread by Galilee;
Then shall all bondage cease, all fetters fall,
And I shall find my peace, my all in all.

Mary A. Lathbury (1841–1913)

The classic hymn "Day Is Dying in the West" was written by Mary
Ann Lathbury for the Chautauqua Conference in New York State in
1877: "Day is dying in the west, / Heaven is touching earth with rest.
/ Wait and worship while the night / Sets her evening lamps alight /
Through all the sky." This is among the most beautiful hymns on the
subject of death. "Break Thou the Bread of Life" was written for the
Bible studies at the Chautauqua meetings.

Jesus once cited Deuteronomy 8:3 saying, "One does not live by bread alone, but by every word that comes from the mouth of God" (Matthew 4:4 NRSV). This verse is quoted among Christians frequently. Yet, ask yourself, "Am I willing to live by the nourishment of God's Word?" Or would you have been among those who were offended when Jesus declared himself to be the bread of life (see John 6:35)?

These people asked each other, "How can this man give us his flesh to eat?" (v. 52). Jesus gave them the answer: "It is the spirit that gives life; the flesh is useless. The words that I have spoken to you are spirit and life" (v. 63). And many turned away from him.

We hope that we would not be like these people who turned away. But the Word of God is really an acquired taste. Jeremiah wrote, "Your words were found, and I ate them, and your words became to me a joy and the delight of my heart" (15:16). Be like Jeremiah and read and pray over the words of the Bible until you find God's words for yourself. Then you will honestly declare, "How sweet are your words to my taste, sweeter than honey to my mouth" (Psalm 119:103). And you will find yourself in the dilemma of the disciples who, when faced with a choice of leaving the Lord said, "To whom can we go? You have the words of eternal life" (John 6:68).

RELATED SCRIPTURE READING—*Psalm 119:41-43*

Lord, because you have given to me your unfailing love, the salvation that you promised, I have an answer for those who scoff at me. I trust in your Word; thank you for the life that comes from it. Always give me this bread of life. Never remove your word of truth from me. It is my only hope.

69

Savior, Teach Me Day by Day

Savior, teach me day by day
Love's sweet lesson to obey,
Sweeter lesson cannot be,
Loving him who first loved me.

With a child's glad heart of love
At Thy bidding may I move,
Prompt to serve and follow thee,
Loving him who first loved me.

Teach me thus thy steps to trace,
Strong to follow in thy grace,
Learning how to love from thee,
Loving him who first loved me.

Love in loving finds employ,
In obedience all her joy;
Ever new that joy will be,
Loving him who first loved me.

Thus may I rejoice to show
That I feel the love I owe;
Singing, till Thy face I see,
Of his love who first loved me.

Jane Eliza Leeson (1807-1882)

A native of London, England, Leeson was active in the Apostolic Catholic Church where some of her hymns were improvised during worship services and considered to be prophetic utterances. She published several books of hymns especially for children, and her translations from the Latin appeared in *Catholic Hymns Arranged in Order for the Principal Festivals, Feasts of Saints, and Other Occasions of Devotion throughout the Year* (1851). Among these translations is "Christ the Lord Is Risen Today."

ere is an idea for the title of a self-help book: *How I Learned to Stop Loving Money and Start Loving Jesus.*

This is a serious topic. Here is how the gospel presents a believer's dichotomy—the conflict between two opposing forces for the possession of your heart. "No one can serve two masters," it says. "For you will hate one and love the other, or be devoted to one and despise the other" (Matthew 6:24 NLT).

"Well," you may respond, "that's not my problem. I don't love the Devil!" Of course you don't. But the gospel does not say that God and Satan are in contention over your heart. Rather it warns, "You cannot serve both God and money" (v. 24).

The epistles describe servants of money: "People who long to be rich fall into temptation and are trapped by many foolish and harmful desires that plunge them into ruin and destruction. For the love of money is at the root of all kinds of evil. And some people, craving money, have wandered from the faith and pierced themselves with many sorrows" (1 Timothy 6:9–10). What a great, piercing sorrow it must be to wander from the faith. The love of money can lead you down that path.

The god of this world is personified as Mammon—money. The world is infected with its worship. As an antidote 1 Timothy continues: "Pursue a godly life, along with faith, love, perseverance, and gentleness. . . . Hold tightly to the eternal life that God has given you, . . . Then no one can find fault with you from now until our Lord Jesus Christ returns" (1 Timothy 6:11, 12, 14). Remember, a prize awaits—"the crown of righteousness that the Lord, the righteous Judge, will give me on that great day of his return" (2 Timothy 4:8).

RELATED SCRIPTURE READING—*Matthew 6:25–34*

Lord, I sometimes worry about food, drink, clothes, and housing. But I know that life consists of more than these things. Remind me to look at the birds. They don't need to plant or harvest or put food in barns, because you feed them. Always remind me that I am far more valuable to you than they are. Forgive me for my worries. They cannot add a single moment to my life.

71

The Lord Bless Thee and Keep Thee

The Lord bless thee and keep thee;
The Lord make his face to shine upon thee,
    and be gracious unto thee,
    and be gracious unto thee;
The Lord lift up his countenance,
    his countenance upon thee,
    and give thee peace.

Lucy Rider Meyer (1849-1922)—Composer

Born near Middlebury, Vermont, Lucy Rider was educated in public schools and, while still a teen, taught in the high school at Brandon, Vermont, and in a school for freedmen at Greensboro, North Carolina. She entered the Junior class at Oberlin College in Ohio, became engaged to a medical missionary, and enrolled in the Women's Medical School in Philadelphia. When her fiancé died she became a high school principal, then a college chemistry professor, and eventually taught at Northfield Academy, Massachusetts. Ms. Rider married Josiah Meyer, a Methodist Episcopal minister, and they opened the Chicago Training School for City, Home, and Foreign Missions where she served as principal until 1917.

God once told Moses, "You cannot see my face; for no one shall see me and live" (Exodus 33:20 NRSV). Yet, later Moses prayed, "The LORD make his face to shine upon you, and be gracious to you" (Numbers 6:25). The question here is, if the sight of God's face brings death, how can the shining of God's face be a coming of grace? The answer: Moses' prayer has been answered in the New Testament. In this age, God has been gracious to us in the Son (see John 1:14).

The presence of God was judgment to those who lived in the days of the Old Testament, because, as Romans says, "all, both Jews and Greeks, are under the power of sin" (3:9). The New Testament records the coming of the Savior, Jesus, who "suffered for sins once for all, the righteous for the unrighteous, in order to bring [us] to God" (1 Peter 3:18). He bore God's judgment so that everyone can enjoy the graceful shining of God's face.

Paul once saw "a light from heaven, brighter than the sun" (Acts 26:13). He is qualified to tell us about the shining face of God. Here is what he says: "The god of this world has blinded the minds of the unbelievers, to keep them from seeing the light of the gospel of the glory of Christ, who is the image of God. . . . For it is the God who said, 'Let light shine out of darkness,' who has shone in our hearts to give the light of the knowledge of the glory of God in the face of Jesus Christ" (2 Corinthians 4:4, 6).

Lucy Rider Meyer composed the musical setting for the benediction still used in churches today. Its words are so comforting to believers because we need never fear God. We can see the light of the knowledge of the glory of God in the face of Jesus Christ.

RELATED SCRIPTURE READING—*John 1:3-5*

O God, hear my prayer for the people who don't believe, who are unable to see the glorious light of the good news that is shining upon them. Open their hearts to understand the message about the glory of your Son, who is made in your likeness. Command the light of the brightness of your glory, seen in the face of Jesus, to shine into human hearts.

Sweeter As the Years Go By

Of Jesus' love that sought me, when I was lost in sin;
Of wondrous grace that brought me back to his fold again;
Of heights and depths of mercy, far deeper than the sea,
And higher than the heavens, my theme shall ever be.

    Sweeter as the years go by, sweeter as the years go by,
    Richer, fuller, deeper, Jesus' love is sweeter,
    Sweeter as the years go by.

He trod in old Judea life's pathway long ago;
The people thronged about him, his saving grace to know;
He healed the broken-hearted, and caused the blind to see;
And still his great heart yearneth in love for even me.

'Twas wondrous love which led him for us to suffer loss,
To bear without a murmur the anguish of the cross;
With saints redeemed in glory, let us our voices raise,
Till heav'n and earth re-echo with our Redeemer's praise.

Lelia Naylor Morris (1862-1929)

Lelia Morris became a Christian at the Martin Lake (Methodist) Camp Meeting in Maryland. She wrote both the words and music to "Nearer, Still Nearer," "The Everlasting Arms," "Sweeter As the Years Go By," and others. About fifteen years before her death Morris began to lose her eyesight; her son built a large blackboard, twenty-eight feet long, complete with staff lines, so she could continue to compose music.

ow do you understand the Lord's love? Do you measure it by the material blessings you have received? Maybe you seek his love in spiritual things—gifts and benefits attributed to the Holy Spirit. Or perhaps you think the way others treat you is an accurate reflection of God's love for you.

Have you ever looked for divine love in the Scripture?

Some people have plenty of money and possessions; others are poor. Some believers seem to be gifted in faith or abilities; others seem ordinary, not spiritual at all. Some people appear to be surrounded by loving family and understanding friends. Many are friendless, betrayed, alone. But all of us have one thing in common—the message of the gospel as recorded in the Bible. Nowhere else can we see and understand the Lord's love.

Here is what Scripture says, "Jesus knew that his hour had come to depart from this world. . . . Having loved his own who were in the world, he loved them to the end" (John 13:1 NRSV). When was the end? When he was crucified. How did Jesus love you? By giving himself for you in death on the cross (see Galatians 2:20).

Why did he have to die for you? Here's why: The human race, including you, fell away from God, left God behind. This separation is called sin. But Christ's death paid the debt of sin and brought you into the grace of God. This is how Scripture describes Jesus' love.

And this is why Lelia Morris sings, "Of Jesus' love that sought me, when I was lost in sin; / Of wondrous grace that brought me back to his fold again; / Of heights and depths of mercy, far deeper than the sea, / And higher than the heavens, my theme shall ever be."

RELATED SCRIPTURE READING—*Hebrews 13:1*

O Son of Man, you came to save the lost. Thank you for finding me and enfolding me into your love. Find a way into the hearts of my friends and loved ones and fellow workers. Please uplift in me your testimony of love, not so much in what I say but in how I live.

One There Is above All Others

One there is above all others, Oh, how he loves!
His is love beyond a brother's, Oh, how he loves!
Earthly friends may fail or leave us, one day soothe, the next day grieve
    us;
But this friend will ne'er deceive us: Oh, how he loves!

'Tis eternal life to know him, Oh, how he loves!
Think, oh, think, how much we owe him, Oh, how he loves!
With his precious blood he bought us, in the wilderness he sought us,
To his flock he safely brought us: Oh, how he loves!

Blessed Jesus! Would you know him? Oh, how he loves!
Give yourselves entirely to him, Oh, how he loves!
Think no longer of the morrow, from the past new courage borrow,
Jesus carries all your sorrow: Oh, how he loves!

All your sins shall be forgiven, Oh, how he loves!
Backward shall your foes be driven, Oh, how he loves!
Blest of blessings he'll provide you, naught but good shall e'er betide
    you,
Safe to glory he will guide you: Oh, how he loves!

Marianne Nunn (1778-1847)

Marianne Nunn wrote *The Benevolent Merchant* and other books.
Her hymn appeared in *Psalms and Hymns from the Most Approved
Authors* (1817), which was published by her brother John Nunn,
Domestic Chaplain to the Earl of Galloway. It later appeared in *Lyra
Britannica* (1867) and in modified form in other hymnals.

Marianne Nunn writes, "Naught but good shall e'er betide you." Let's think about this. Don't things happen to you that seem less than good? But Romans 8 says, "We know that God causes everything to work together for the good of those who love God and are called according to his purpose for them" (v. 28 NLT).

Reading this, one may think, *Some things in my life are not working out for good. Maybe I'm not in God's purpose.* Please don't think this way. Instead, look at Scripture.

Romans 8:27 says, ". . . the Spirit pleads for us believers in harmony with God's own will." Astounding! The Holy Spirit is praying for you. And naturally this prayer is in harmony with God's will—because the Spirit is God!

Next, verse 28 says that everything is for the good. Here's a thought: "Whose good is this verse talking about?" We propose to you that everything works out for *God's* good—so that he can accomplish the divine purpose.

The next logical question is, what is God's purpose for your life? A certain career? Marriage? Read verse 29—"God knew his people in advance, and he chose them to become like his Son, so that his Son would be the firstborn, with many brothers and sisters."

God's purpose for you is the same as that for every Christian who ever lived—to make you like the Son in all things except his divinity.

As John wrote, "Yes, dear friends, we are already God's children, and we can't even imagine what we will be like when Christ returns. But we do know that when he comes we will be like him, for we will see him as he really is" (1 John 3:2).

RELATED SCRIPTURE READING—*Colossians 1:15-18*

Thank you, dear God! Because of Christ I am one of your children. I can't even imagine what I will be like when Christ returns. But I do know, because of your promises, that when he comes I will be like him. So I pray that I would not despise the difficulties and sufferings of this life. I only ask that you would use them for the fulfillment of your purpose.

Jesus Saves!

We have heard the joyful sound: Jesus saves! Jesus saves!
Spread the tidings all around: Jesus saves! Jesus saves!
Bear the news to every land, climb the steeps and cross the waves;
Onward! 'tis our Lord's command; Jesus saves! Jesus saves!

Waft it on the rolling tide: Jesus saves! Jesus saves!
Tell to sinners far and wide: Jesus saves! Jesus saves!
Sing, you islands of the sea; echo back, you ocean caves;
Earth shall keep her jubilee: Jesus saves! Jesus saves!

Sing above the battle strife: Jesus saves! Jesus saves!
By His death and endless life, Jesus saves! Jesus saves!
Sing it softly through the gloom, when the heart for mercy craves;
Sing in triumph o'er the tomb: Jesus saves! Jesus saves!

Give the winds a mighty voice: Jesus saves! Jesus saves!
Let the nations now rejoice: Jesus saves! Jesus saves!
Shout salvation full and free; highest hills and deepest caves;
This our song of victory: Jesus saves! Jesus saves!

Priscilla Jane Owens (1829-1907)

For forty-nine years Priscilla Owens was a public school teacher
and Sunday school teacher in Baltimore, Maryland. She is also the
author of "Will Your Anchor Hold?" "Jesus Saves!" has appeared in
many hymnals and is sung with joy to this day.

In the foothills of the White Mountains, on Route 110 heading west out of Berlin, New Hampshire, someone recently erected in their yard a slender cross, ten or fifteen feet tall. One night we were driving through the mountain darkness, and this cross, brightly lit, suddenly appeared at the top of a rise in the road.

Such displays of faith may be common in America's so-called Bible Belt. But not in northern New England. In other places it may even still be common to see the words *Jesus Saves!* crudely painted on large roadside rocks.

Most of us neither paint rocks nor erect crosses. Nor do we have the opportunity to waft the gospel on the rolling tide in order to tell it to sinners far and wide. We probably don't have the personality or disposition for this. But that's all right. Don't think you are lacking in zeal. Instead, consider how the apostle Paul spread the gospel.

"Wherever we go [God] uses us to tell others about the Lord and to spread the Good News like a sweet perfume. Our lives are a fragrance presented by Christ to God. But this fragrance is perceived differently by those being saved and by those perishing. To those who are perishing we are a fearful smell of death and doom. But to those who are being saved we are a life-giving perfume" (2 Corinthians 2:14–16 NLT).

A normal way to tell others you believe in Jesus Christ—more normal than say, painting on rocks—is to patiently allow people to sense Christ in your life. Let him tell others for you, "Jesus saves!"

RELATED SCRIPTURE READING—*Numbers 15:1-3*

Heavenly Father, save me from becoming like those who preach for their own benefit and bank account. Allow me instead to present your message with the sincerity and prestige of Christ. I know that if you sent me, you are also observing me. So please, have mercy on me and my testimony.

Jesus! I Am Resting, Resting

Jesus! I am resting, resting in the joy of what thou art;
I am finding out the greatness of thy loving heart.
Thou hast bid me gaze upon thee, and thy beauty fills my soul,
For, by thy transforming power, thou hast made me whole.

Oh, how great thy loving kindness, vaster, broader than the sea;
Oh, how marvelous thy goodness, lavished all on me!
Yes, I rest in thee, beloved, know what wealth of grace is thine,
Know thy certainty of promise, and have made it mine.

Simply trusting thee, Lord Jesus, I behold thee as thou art,
And thy love, so pure, so changeless, satisfies my heart,
Satisfies its deepest longings, meets, supplies its every need,
Compasseth me round with blessings, thine is love indeed.

Ever lift thy face upon me as I work and wait for thee;
Resting 'neath thy smile, Lord Jesus, earth's dark shadows flee.
Brightness of my Father's glory, sunshine of my Father's face,
Keep me ever trusting, resting, fill me with thy grace.

Jean Sophia Pigott (1845-1882)

The Keswick Convention at Brighton, England, has had profound spiritual effect on many Christians, among them Jean Sophia Pigott. Ms. Pigott was born in Ireland and after 1875 was an invalid. She not only wrote the above hymn, it is said that she lived according to its sentiments. Two of her brothers were missionaries to China, one a martyr. Pigott was a hymnist, composer, and artist.

It is said that this was the favorite hymn of James Hudson Taylor (1832–1905). Dr. Taylor sailed as a missionary to China in 1853. He was the first among the Lord's workers there to adopt the dress and lifestyle of the people to whom he was sent. He severed his ties to the evangelistic societies in England because of their financial policies and set forth entirely by faith to bring the gospel to the unimaginably expansive interior of China. Not only had this never been attempted, it had never even been considered and, at that time, it was illegal for foreigners to travel to inland China.

Taylor depended entirely on the Lord's goodness for funds to finance the China Inland Mission. He would not allow any public appeals for financial support. Instead he and his fellow workers appealed directly to God. The work was very much blessed, and whatever Christian vitality exists today in China must be due in great part to the pioneering work of Hudson Taylor.

The life and work of this man is a lesson in financial responsibility in the ministry. He chose the safe and blessed road of trial rather than the alternative way of debt and appeals to man. He once wrote in a letter: "I am truly sorry that you should be distressed at not having funds to send me. After living on God's faithfulness for many years, I can testify that times of want have ever been times of special blessing, or have led to them. I do beg that never any appeal for funds be put forward, save to God in prayer. When our work becomes a begging work, it dies. God is faithful, must be so. He has said: 'Take *no* thought (anxiety) for your life, what ye shall eat, or what ye shall drink.' It is doubting, beloved brother, not trusting that is tempting the Lord."

RELATED SCRIPTURE READING—*1 Corinthians 2:9*

Lord Jesus, may I simply trust you for all things, and then I will see you as you really are. I want to allow your love, which I know is so pure and so changeless, to satisfy my heart. Satisfy its deepest longings, meet and supply its every need, and surround me with your true blessings. Yours is love indeed!

Have Thine Own Way, Lord!

Have thine own way, Lord! Have thine own way!
Thou art the potter, I am the clay.
Mold me and make me after thy will,
While I am waiting, yielded and still.

Have thine own way, Lord! Have thine own way!
Search me and try me, master, today!
Whiter than snow, Lord, wash me just now,
As in thy presence humbly I bow.

Have thine own way, Lord! Have thine own way!
Wounded and weary, help me, I pray!
Power, all power, surely is thine!
Touch me and heal me, Savior divine.

Have thine own way, Lord! Have thine own way!
Hold o'er my being absolute sway!
Fill with thy Spirit till all shall see
Christ only, always, living in me.

Adelaide Addison Pollard (1862-1934)

Pollard was born in Iowa and attended schools there, in Indiana, and in Massachusetts. In the 1880s she taught in girls' schools in Chicago and later at the Missionary Training School in Nyack, New York. Before and during World War I, Pollard served as a missionary in Africa and Scotland. She died in New York City.

Adelaide Potter was certain that the Lord wanted her to be a missionary to Africa. But when she set out to raise funds for this purpose, she was unsuccessful. This, understandably, put her into an uncertain state of mind. In this condition, Potter attended a prayer meeting where she heard an elderly woman pray: "It's all right, Lord. It doesn't matter what you bring into our lives, just have your own way with us."

Potter returned home much encouraged and began to write: "Have thine own way, Lord! Have thine own way! / Thou art the potter, I am the clay. / Mold me and make me after thy will, / While I am waiting, yielded and still."

This is a wonderful hymn to sing anytime. But it is especially comforting in times of change and insecurity. When Adelaide Potter heard the woman pray, "Have your own way," she was hearing one of the oldest prayers of the New Testament era.

The Lord gave us a pattern of prayer in Matthew 6. We call this the Lord's Prayer and use it frequently. But the Lord gave us another, more personal example of prayer at the end of Matthew: "My Father!" he prayed. "If it is possible, may this cup be taken from me. Yet not as I will, but as you will" (26:39 NIV). Jesus repeated this prayer two more times (vv. 42, 44).

This is the prayer Ms. Potter heard at that prayer meeting and enlarged and embellished into today's beautiful hymn. Many Christians recite the Lord's Prayer every Sunday in a church service. But this other prayer of the Lord can be effectively prayed every day of your life.

RELATED SCRIPTURE READING—*Romans 12:1-2*

O God, I give my body to you. Make it a living and holy sacrifice—the kind you will accept. When I think of what you have done for me, this is not too much to ask. And, dear God, transform me by changing the way I think. Then I will know what you want me to do, and I will know how good and pleasing and perfect your will really is.

More Love to Thee, O Christ

More love to thee, O Christ, more love to thee!
Hear thou the prayer I make on bended knee;
This is my earnest plea: More love, O Christ, to thee,
More love to thee, more love to thee!

Let sorrow do its work, come grief or pain;
Sweet are thy messengers, sweet their refrain,
When they can sing with me: More love, O Christ, to thee,
More love to thee, more love to thee!

Then shall my latest breath whisper thy praise;
This be the parting cry my heart shall raise,
This still its prayer shall be: More love, O Christ, to thee,
More love to thee, more love to thee!

Elizabeth Prentiss (1818-1878)

This fifth of eight children was born in Portland, Maine, and at age sixteen her poetry began to be published. She taught school in Portland as well as Ipswich, Massachusetts, and Richmond, Virginia. Married to George L. Prentiss, a Congregational minister, she moved to New York City where he was professor of homiletics and polity at Union Theological Seminary. She was also the author of numerous books including *Stepping Heavenward* (1869).

"My beloved has a vineyard on a rich and fertile hill" (Isaiah 5:1 NLT). These enchanting words introduce the fearful parable in Isaiah 5 whose prophecy was wholly fulfilled. It tells the story of a land that was plowed, cleared of stones, and planted with choice vines. In the middle the vintner "built a watchtower and carved a winepress in the nearby rocks. Then waited for a harvest of sweet grapes, but the grapes that grew were wild and sour" (v. 2).

Isaiah interprets the parable: "This is the story of the LORD's people. They are the vineyard of the LORD Almighty. Israel and Judah are his pleasant garden. He expected them to yield a crop of justice, but instead he found bloodshed. He expected to find righteousness, but instead he heard cries of oppression" (v. 7). As it is written, fearful judgment came upon the Lord's vineyard, Israel (see vv. 5–6).

Let's say you are a vine in that vineyard hearing this parable. And say you are searching the prophets' words for a way to escape the predicted destruction. Your investigation leads you to the images of vines and vineyards in the Song of Solomon. There in chapter seven you discover familiar words: "I am my beloved's, and his desire is for me" (v. 10 NRSV). You read on: "Let us go out early to the vineyards, and see whether the . . . grape blossoms have opened and the pomegranates are in bloom. There I will give you my love" (v. 12). Ah! In the vineyard God hopes to be satisfied by your love!

Then you remember the first and greatest commandment: "You shall love the LORD your God with all your heart . . ." (Deuteronomy 6:5). And you begin to pray with Elizabeth Prentiss—"More love to thee!"

RELATED SCRIPTURE READING—*1 John 4:19-21*

I want to love you more, O Christ! Allow me to let sorrow, grief, and pain do their work. Help me to see them as your messengers. I want to hear their sweet refrain, when they can sing with me and I with them, "More love to you, O Christ, more love to you, more love to you!"

God Who Made the Earth

God who made the earth,
   The air, the sky, the sea,
Who gave the light its birth,
   Careth for me.

God who made the grass,
   The flower, the fruit, the tree,
The day and night to pass,
   Careth for me.

God who made the sun,
   The moon, the stars, is he
Who when life's clouds come on,
   Careth for me.

Sarah Betts Rhodes (1829-1904)

This hymnist, composer, and sculptor was married to a master silversmith of Sheffield, England. She wrote her hymn for the Congregationalist Sheffield Sunday School Union Whitsuntide Festival in 1870. After her husband's death she became head of a girls' school in Notts, England.

This short, sweet hymn recalls the words of James 1:16–17—"Don't be deceived, my dear brothers. Every good and perfect gift is from above, coming down from the Father of the heavenly lights" (NIV). James is concerned that something will mislead us. What do you think this is? In verses 12–15 James suggests that we may think that God sends bad things into our lives. This is not true; this thought is a deceit. As Sarah Rhodes says in her hymn, "God who made the sun, / The moon, the stars, is he / Who when life's clouds come on, / Careth for me."

Yes, God made all heaven's lights, but unlike them he "does not change like shifting shadows" (v. 17). Every day, as the sun and moon rise and set, God is unchanging in the outworking of the divine purpose for humanity—for you and for me. But sometimes in this human life, we "groan and are burdened" (2 Corinthians 5:4).

And so you may moan, "Why is God doing this to me?" Scripture's answer: So that you may be "clothed with [your] heavenly dwelling, so that what is mortal may be swallowed up by life" (v. 4). And it concludes with these encouraging words: "Now it is God who has made us for this very purpose . . ." (v. 5).

James says, "He chose to give us birth" (James 1:18). Praise God, you are a child of God. And so you can, like Ms. Rhodes, proclaim with confidence, "God cares for me." And God, who is unchanging, will continue to care until we grow to become the choice harvest of all creation.

RELATED SCRIPTURE READING—*Psalm 55:22*

Lord, you said that everyone who asks, receives. Everyone who seeks, finds. And the door is opened to everyone who knocks. But help me to remember that if I ask for bread and your answer appears to be a stone instead—you care for me. Or if I ask for a fish, and it seems like I've been given a snake—you care for me.

In the Bleak Midwinter

In the bleak midwinter,
  frosty wind made moan,
Earth stood hard as iron,
  water like a stone;
Snow had fallen, snow on snow,
  snow on snow.
In the bleak midwinter,
  long ago.

Our God, heaven cannot hold him,
  nor earth sustain;
Heaven and earth shall flee away
  when he comes to reign:
In the bleak midwinter
  a stable place sufficed
The Lord God incarnate,
  Jesus Christ.

Angels and archangels
  may have gathered there,
Cherubim and seraphim
  thronged the air;
But his mother only,
  in her maiden bliss,
Worshiped the beloved
  with a kiss.

What can I give him,
  poor as I am?
If I were a shepherd,
  I would bring a lamb;
If I were a wise man,
  I would do my part;
Yet what I can I give him,
  give my heart.

Christina Rossetti (1830–1894)

This English lyric poet was a devout High Church Anglican. Her devotion to God is seen in *Goblin Market and Other Poems* (1862), considered her finest poetry, and *The Prince's Progress and Other Poems* (1866). She was the sister of Dante Gabriel Rossetti, the Pre-Raphaelite painter and poet for whom she posed for several portraits of the Madonna.

Christian scholars generally agree that Jesus Christ was not born in the wintertime. Yet it is still appropriate that we observe the Savior's birth in what is in many regions the darkest and coldest time of the year—the bleak midwinter. In this hymn Christina Rossetti poetically depicts the world before the arrival of Jesus Christ—the Lord God incarnate: "Snow had fallen, snow on snow, snow on snow." Job describes humanity without God in a similar way: "Lacking clothes, they spend the night naked; they have nothing to cover themselves in the cold" (Job 24:7 NIV). And, significantly, on the night of Christ's betrayal "it was cold, and the servants and officials stood around a fire they had made to keep warm" (John 18:18).

Figuratively speaking, people today are still trying to warm themselves around fires they themselves have made—material possessions, personal accomplishments, social position, and so forth. Christina Rossetti's hymn conveys the chill that is upon humanity without God. But it also shows the comfort of loving worship—the kind of worship that angels can only observe from a distance.

Rossetti ends this hymn with a warm thought for all of us who have ever felt lacking in our gifts for God—*Yet what I can I give him, give my heart.*

RELATED SCRIPTURE READING—*Psalm 147:15-20*

Lord, I really don't have much to give you. You are rich; you own the cattle on a thousand hills. What do I have that you can use? I simply present my heart to you. I know that it is only a human heart after all. But your Son lived and died and so captured me, captured my heart. Thank you that because of Jesus Christ, I can give myself to you, and you accept me.

Children of the Heavenly Father

Children of the heavenly Father
Safely in his bosom gather;
Nestling bird nor star in heaven
Such a refuge e'er was given.

God his own doth tend and nourish;
In his holy courts they flourish;
From all evil things he spares them;
In His mighty arms he bears them.

Neither life nor death shall ever
From the Lord his children sever;
Unto them his grace he showeth,
And their sorrows all he knoweth.

Though he giveth or he taketh,
God his children never forsaketh;
His the loving purpose solely
To preserve them pure and holy.

Karolina Wilhelmina Sandell-Berg (1832–1903)

Sometimes called the "Fanny Crosby of Sweden," Sandell wrote more than 650 hymns and lyrics. The music for her hymns was written by Oskar Ahnfelt, who also traveled throughout the Scandinavian countries performing them.

ina Sandell was the daughter of a Lutheran pastor in Fröderyd, Sweden. When she was twenty-six, she accompanied her father, Jonas, on a boat trip to Gothenberg. The boat tipped, and he fell overboard and drowned before his daughter's eyes. This tragedy profoundly shocked Lina, yet inspired her to write hymns. This calamity whispers under the words of today's beautiful hymn.

Its third verse refers to Romans 8:38–39—"For I am convinced that neither death, nor life, . . . nor height, nor depth, nor anything else in all creation, will be able to separate us from the love of God in Christ Jesus our Lord" (NRSV). These words are a continuation of verse 28, well-known to many Christians: "We know that all things work together for good for those who love God, who are called according to his purpose."

The big question is, "What is God's purpose for me?" Of all questions, the Scripture certainly answers this one. In fact, it gives the answer in the next verse—"For those whom he foreknew he also predestined to be conformed to the image of his Son, in order that he might be the firstborn within a large family" (v. 29). God's purpose for your life is the same as it was for Lina Sandell's. That is, that you will match the Son. Why? This is not only for your glory; it is so that God's family will be complete.

In her heartache Ms. Sandell sang, "Though he giveth or he taketh, / God his children never forsaketh; / His the loving purpose solely / To preserve them pure and holy." The Bible says the same thing in this way: "Those whom he predestined he also called; and those whom he called he also justified; and those whom he justified he also glorified" (v. 30).

RELATED SCRIPTURE READING—*Psalm 84:3-4*

O living God! I know that you purpose to preserve me pure and holy. Make me like the sparrow who finds a home in your dwelling place and the swallow who builds her nest and raises her young at a place near your altar. O Lord Almighty, my King and my God! How happy are those who can live in your house, always singing your praises.

It Passeth Knowledge

It passeth knowledge, that dear love of thine,
My Savior, Jesus; yet this soul of mine
Would of thy love in all its breadth and length,
Its height and depth, its everlasting strength,
 Know more and more.

It passeth telling, that dear love of thine,
My Savior, Jesus; yet these lips of mine
Would fain proclaim to sinners, far and near,
A love which can remove all guilty fear,
 And love beget.

It passeth praises, that dear love of thine,
My Savior, Jesus; yet this heart of mine
Would sing that love, so full, so rich, so free,
Which brings a rebel sinner, such as me,
 Nigh unto God.

But though I cannot sing, or tell, or know
The fulness of thy love, while here below,
My empty vessel I may freely bring;
O thou, who are of love the living spring,
 My vessel fill.

Mary Shekleton (1827-1883)

Mary Shekleton's hymn was first published in 1863. One hundred years later it was published in the English *Baptist Hymn Book* and is still popular today. She lived her entire life in Dublin, Ireland.

The King James Version of the Bible says, "And to know the love of Christ, which passeth knowledge, that ye might be filled with all the fulness of God" (Ephesians 3:19). Surely Mary Shekleton was contemplating this verse when writing this hymn.

With Bible studies, sermons, gospel magazines, devotional books, and Christian television and radio broadcasts all around, we would be wise to remember that the love of Christ surpasses all human knowledge—that we cannot sing, or tell, or know the fullness of God's love.

Paul said, "When I think of the wisdom and scope of God's plan, I fall to my knees and pray to the Father, the Creator of everything in heaven and on earth" (Ephesians 3:14–15 NLT). The very thought of God's love reduced the great apostle to prayer. The following is a paraphrase of that prayer. Use it today, this week, this month. Continue to seek God with variations of this prayer. See how it will transform your life.

> Dear heavenly Father, you are the Creator of everything in heaven and on earth. You have glorious, unlimited resources. Please give me mighty inner strength through your Holy Spirit. And I pray that Christ will be more and more at home in my heart as I trust in him. May my roots go down deep into the soil of your marvelous love.
>
> O God, give me the power to understand, together with all your people, how wide, how long, how high, and how deep your love is. Let me experience the love of Christ, though it is so great I will never fully understand it. Fill me with the fullness of your life and power (Eph. 3:14–19).

No, you cannot sing, or tell, or know the fullness of God's love, while here below. But in prayer you can bring your empty vessel to God, who is the living spring of love, and pray, "My vessel fill."

RELATED SCRIPTURE READING—*2 Corinthians 4:6-7*

> Lord, I don't want to worry about anything; instead, turn me to pray about everything and remind me to thank you for all you have done. You promise to give me your peace, which is far more wonderful than the human mind can understand. I want your peace, Lord. Let it guard my heart and mind as I live in you.

Father, Whate'er of Earthly Bliss

Father, whate'er of earthly bliss
    Thy sov'reign will denies,
Accepted at thy throne of grace
    Let this petition rise:

Give me a calm and thankful heart,
    From ev'ry murmur free;
The blessings of thy grace impart,
    And make me live to thee.

Let the firm hope that thou art mine
    My path of life attend:
Thy presence through my journey shine,
    And crown my journey's end.

Anne Steele (1716-1778)

Steele's fiancé was drowned a few hours before they were to be married. She never fully recovered from the shock of this tragedy. Her first book of devotional poems was published in 1760 under the pseudonym *Theodosia*. Later editions were published in England in 1780 and in America in 1808. Others of her poems were published only under the name *Steele*. But in 1863, 144 of her poems were published in *Hymns, Psalms, and Poems by Anne Steele*.

nne Steele's hymn suggests that she knew suffering. She was always of delicate health and suffered even more when the man she was to marry drowned on their wedding day. This hymn tells how she prayed. Especially striking is the line, "The blessings of thy grace impart, and make me live to thee."

She asked for a calm and thankful heart. She desired the Lord's presence, not his miraculous healing. She seems to have learned from the apostle Paul, who suffered with what he called "a thorn in my flesh." Three different times he begged the Lord to take it away. Each time the Lord said, "My grace is sufficient for you, for my power is made perfect in weakness" (2 Corinthians 12:9 NIV).

Paul had to learn this lesson the hard way. He prayed three times and got no answer. He had healed others, but he could not heal himself. Anne Steele lost her love on their wedding day. Such an experience surely affected every day of the remainder of her life. A thorn in her flesh.

Some of us have lost a child or a spouse to sickness or accident. Some have experienced the pain of divorce, abuse, or abandonment; illness, disease, or handicap. Such painful experiences can become persistent, daily thorns in the flesh, no less disturbing than Paul's or Anne's.

If you have such pain, remember that the Bible is not a book of theory and the Christian faith is not a philosophy. Jesus Christ *has* enacted the new covenant with God. This is the covenant of grace. If God told Paul, "My grace is sufficient for you," do you think that he would reply to your prayers any differently? This is doubtful. Instead, draw on the inexhaustible well of God's grace.

RELATED SCRIPTURE READING—*Acts 20:32*

O God of grace, I give thanks for all I have from you. Grace wrote my name in the Book of Life. Grace gave me to the Lamb who took all my sorrows. Grace taught my wandering feet to walk on the pilgrim road and supplies me for this journey to you. And thank you too that grace taught my heart to pray and will not let me go.

Still, Still with Thee

Still, still with thee, when purple morning breaketh,
When the bird waketh, and the shadows flee;
Fairer than morning, lovelier than daylight,
Dawns the sweet consciousness, I am with thee.

Still, still with thee! As to each newborn morning
A fresh and solemn splendor still is given,
So does this blessed consciousness, awaking,
Breathe each day nearness unto thee and heaven.

When sinks the soul, subdued by toil, to slumber,
Its closing eyes look up to thee in prayer;
Sweet the repose beneath thy wings o'ershading,
But sweeter still, to wake and find thee there.

So shall it be at last, in that bright morning,
When the soul waketh, and life's shadows flee;
O in that hour, fairer than daylight dawning,
Shall rise the glorious thought, I am with thee.

Harriet Beecher Stowe (1811-1896)

Stowe's novel *Uncle Tom's Cabin* was published in 1852. It sold ten thousand copies in the first week, phenomenal for mid-nineteenth-century America. The influence of this book effectively promoted anti-slavery and issues related to the Civil War. Stowe also wrote *Footsteps of the Master* and many hymns. These were published by her brother, Henry Ward Beecher, in the 1865 edition of the *Plymouth Collection*.

I n the ancient Roman military, nighttime guard duty was broken up into four three-hour time periods from 6 P.M. to 6 A.M. The final period was called the morning watch. This term has also been used by Christians to designate a time of prayer in the early morning. As Harriet Beecher Stowe describes in her hymn, the morning watch can be truly wonderful.

But her hymn is about more than awakening for morning prayer. It concerns that bright morning "when the soul waketh, and life's shadows flee"—the day of resurrection.

What happens when we die? According to Scripture, death is like falling asleep. Lazarus had been dead for three days when Jesus said, "Our friend Lazarus has fallen asleep, but I am going there to wake him up" (John 11:11 NIV). And 1 Corinthians 15, the definitive chapter on the resurrection of the dead, refers to death as sleep four times. For example, concerning Christ it says, "But Christ has indeed been raised from the dead, the firstfruits of those who have fallen asleep" (v. 20).

What then is the Christian's hope? The sweet resurrection morning of which Ms. Stowe sings. "We believe that Jesus died and rose again and so we believe that God will bring with Jesus those who have fallen asleep in him" (1 Thessalonians 4:13). We know that the fresh morning will come when "the Lord himself will come down from heaven, . . . and the dead in Christ will rise first" (1 Thessalonians 4:16). Hallelujah!

RELATED SCRIPTURE READING—*John 11:25-26*

Glory to thee, my God, this night / For all the blessings of the light; / Keep me, O keep me, King of kings, / Beneath thy own almighty wings. // Teach me to live, that I may dread / The grave as little as my bed; / Teach me to die, that so I may / Rise glorious at the awful day (from the poem "Glory to Thee, My God, This Night" by Thomas Ken—1637–1711).

Savior, like a Shepherd Lead Us

Savior, like a shepherd lead us, much we need thy tender care;
In thy pleasant pastures feed us, for our use thy folds prepare:
    Blessed Jesus, Blessed Jesus! Thou hast bought us, thine we are;
    Blessed Jesus, Blessed Jesus! Thou hast bought us, thine we are.

We are thine, do thou befriend us, be the guardian of our way;
Keep thy flock, from sin defend us, seek us when we go astray:
    Blessed Jesus, Blessed Jesus! Hear, O hear us, when we pray;
    Blessed Jesus, Blessed Jesus! Hear, O hear us, when we pray.

Thou hast promised to receive us, poor and sinful though we be;
Thou hast mercy to relieve us, grace to cleanse, and power to free:
    Blessed Jesus, Blessed Jesus! Early let us turn to thee,
    Blessed Jesus, Blessed Jesus! Early let us turn to thee.

Early let us seek thy favor, early let us do thy will;
Blessed Lord and only Savior, with thy love our bosoms fill:
    Blessed Jesus, Blessed Jesus! Thou hast loved us, love us still,
    Blessed Jesus, Blessed Jesus! Thou hast loved us, love us still.

Dorothy A. Thrupp (1779-1847)

Born in London, Thrupp contributed hymns under the pseudonym *Iota* to W. C. Wilson's *Friendly Visitor* and his *Children's Friend*. The *Selection of Hymns and Poetry for Use of Infants and Juvenile Schools and Families* (1838) contained hymns by Ms. Thrupp under the initials D.A.T. She was the editor of *Hymns for the Young* (c. 1830) to which all the hymns were given anonymously.

orothy Thrupp writes, "Blessed Jesus! Thou hast bought us, thine we are." She drew this beautiful thought from a section of the New Testament that mentions slavery (see 1 Corinthians 7:17–24). Here Paul did not openly condemn slavery. Instead he wrote, "You must accept whatever situation the Lord has put you in, and continue on as you were when God first called you" (v. 17 NLT). Paul is criticized for this.

But we must remember that God gave Paul the singular task of laying the foundation of the Christian faith (see 1 Corinthians 3:10–11). Out of this faith would rise nations and societies that would abolish slavery and elevate the human condition. Paul was not called to be a social reformer. He was a skilled master builder of the church of God.

A key footing in faith's foundation is the fact that we walk by faith, not sight. In the Christian faith such symbols and marks as circumcision and uncircumcision mean nothing (see 1 Corinthians 7:19). The New Testament also mentions the ancient ranks of slave and freeman, rigid social positions. But a person's status in the faith is not concerned with this (see v. 21). Religious marks and social status are matters of sight—of appearance. But Christians live by faith.

Scripture concludes that we were bought with a price and shouldn't be enslaved by the world. People who place undue value on outward appearances and social position are enslaved to the world. But God purchased us with the price of the death of Jesus Christ and so has received us, "poor and sinful though we be." Pray that the world will receive such mercy and grace. The more it does this, the more we will witness the eradication of oppression.

RELATED SCRIPTURE READING—*Philemon 10-16*

How I praise you, God, the Father of my Lord Jesus Christ. You have blessed me with every spiritual blessing because I belong to him. I praise you for your kindness in purchasing my freedom through the blood of your Son. Thank you that at the right time, you will bring everything together under the authority of Christ—everything in heaven and on earth.

We Would See Jesus

We would see Jesus; for the shadows lengthen
    Across this little landscape of our life;
We would see Jesus; our weak faith to strengthen
    For the last weariness, the final strife.

We would see Jesus; the great rock foundation
    Whereon our feet were set by sovereign grace:
Not life nor death, with all their agitation,
    Can thence remove us, if we see his face.

We would see Jesus; other lights are paling,
    Which for long years we have rejoiced to see;
The blessings of our pilgrimage are failing:
    We would not mourn them, for we go to thee.

We would see Jesus; this is all we're needing;
    Strength, joy, and willingness come with the sight;
We would see Jesus, dying, risen, pleading;
    Then welcome day, and farewell mortal night.

Anna Bartlett Warner (1821–1915)

Anna Warner lived with her sister, Susan, on Constitution Island opposite West Point in the Hudson River. They conducted Bible studies for the Cadets at the U.S. Military Academy at West Point. Anna may be best remembered for the song, "Jesus Loves Me, This I Know." She wrote two volumes of hymns: *Hymns of the Church Militant* (1848) and *Wayfaring Hymns, Original and Translated* (1869).

Reading this hymn I think of my maternal grandmother. In the midst of her ninth decade of life she lay in a nursing home in Manhattan, Kansas. The shadows had lengthened across the little landscape of her life. Nearly a century before, she had been carried west by wagon during the final great expansion of this country. When I last saw her, the blessings of her pilgrimage were failing.

She was well-liked by the staff of the home because she did not complain. Often when asked, "And how are you today?" my grandmother would answer, "I have learned the secret . . . of having plenty and of being in need" (Philippians 4:12 NRSV).

Today's hymn sings of that secret.

As I grow older, I wonder, like the pondering psalmist, "What are human beings . . . that you care for them?" The Book of Hebrews quotes this verse and goes on, "You have made them for a little while lower than the angels; you have crowned them with glory and honor, subjecting all things under their feet" (Hebrews 2:6–8).

The psalmist was wondering, "What is life all about?" Countless folks facing the end of life have asked this same question. Hebrews continues: "As it is, we do not yet see everything in subjection to them" (v. 8). In other words, "This world's a mess!" Then it reveals my grandmother's secret—"but we do see Jesus who for a little while was made lower than the angels, now crowned with glory and honor because of the suffering of death, so that by the grace of God he might taste death for everyone" (v. 9).

"We would see Jesus, dying, risen, pleading; / Then welcome day, and farewell mortal night."

RELATED SCRIPTURE READING—*John 20:24-28*

O Lord, even though I have never seen you, I love you. This love makes me happy with a glorious, inexpressible joy. And Lord, though I do not see you, I have faith in you. Faith is my confident assurance that what I hope for is going to happen. Thank you for giving me faith, hope, and love.

Not I, But Christ

Not I, but Christ be honored, loved, exalted,
Not I, but Christ be seen, be known and heard;
Not I, but Christ in every look and action,
Not I, but Christ in ev'ry thought and word.

   Oh, to be saved from myself, dear Lord,
   Oh, to be lost in thee,
   Oh, that it may be no more I,
   But Christ that lives in me.

Not I, but Christ to gently soothe in sorrow,
Not I, but Christ to wipe the falling tear;
Not I, but Christ to lift the weary burden,
Not I, but Christ to hush away all fear.

Christ, only Christ, no idle word e'er falling,
Christ, only Christ, no needless bustling sound;
Christ, only Christ, no self-important bearing,
Christ, only Christ, no trace of I be found.

Not I, but Christ my every need supplying,
Not I, but Christ my strength and health to be;
Christ, only Christ, for spirit, soul, and body,
Christ, only Christ, live then thy life in me.

Christ, only Christ, ere long will fill my vision,
Glory excelling soon, full soon I'll see;
Christ, only Christ, my every wish fulfilling,
Christ, only Christ, my all in all to be.

Ada Anne Whiddington (1855-1933)

Little is known of Ada Whittington save that she was born in England. Whiddington's son was Cavendish Professor of Physics at Cambridge University.

Elders in the early church at Jerusalem presented the apostle Paul with the following problem: The church had been told that Paul taught the Jews to forsake the observance of the law. This was not true. But the elders were concerned that, because of this misunderstanding, Paul's presence in Jerusalem would cause an uproar in the church (see Acts 21:21–22).

Jewish law carefully circumscribed diet, but Gentiles ate almost anything. So Paul wrote, "Food will not bring us close to God" (1 Corinthians 8:8 NRSV). Believers have the freedom to eat however they wish—kosher or not, vegetarian or not. God doesn't care. God wants your faith in Christ. But in the present case, Paul was careful that his liberty did not cause the Jewish Christians to stumble (v. 9).

So he joined four members of the church in Jerusalem in a religious rite (see Acts 21:23–26). Paul was not attempting to please God by performing this rite. But he was sympathetic to the elders' fellowship and to the sensibilities of Jewish believers. Please note: Paul was no worse off for participating in the rite, and the men who joined him were no better. Their only benefit before God was their common faith in Jesus.

What does this have to do with today's hymn? For salvation into eternal life, your accomplishments, abilities, diet, laws, regulations, denomination, race, color, gender, and national origin mean nothing. As the hymnist writes, "Christ, only Christ, no trace of I be found."

RELATED SCRIPTURE READING—*Matthew 17:1-8*

Lord, I pray that you will teach me more deeply that I am right with you, not by doing what some law commands, but by faith in Jesus Christ. Thank you that you accept me because of my faith in Christ and not because I have followed some principles or laws. Praise you! I no longer live, but Christ lives in me. So I live my life in this earthly body by trusting in the Son of God, who loved me and gave himself for me.

All My Life Long I Had Panted

All my life long I had panted
For a draft from some cool spring,
That I hoped would quench the burning
Of the thirst I felt within.

Hallelujah! I have found him whom my soul so long has craved!
Jesus satisfies my longings; through his blood I now am saved.

Feeding on the husks around me,
Till my strength was almost gone,
Longed my soul for something better,
Only still to hunger on.

Poor I was, and sought for riches,
Something that would satisfy,
But the dust I gathered round me
Only mocked my soul's sad cry.

Well of water, ever springing,
Bread of life, so rich and free,
Untold wealth that never faileth,
My Redeemer is to me.

Clara Tear Williams (1858-1937)

Williams wrote hymns and was consulting editor for *Sacred Hymns and Tunes Designed for Use in the Wesleyan Methodist Connection* (1900). She lived in retirement in Houghton, New York, which was also the home of Christian vocalist George Beverly Shea. He once reflected that the appearance of Ms. Williams reminded him of the painting "Whistler's Mother" and that he enjoyed "the soft, musical tones of her voice."

e who have found satisfaction in Christ will do well to sing this hymn from time to time in order to remember our past thirst—"All my life long I had panted for a draft from some cool spring." And don't you still experience a soul-thirst from time to time? This is a longing that cannot be quenched at shopping malls or sporting events, through drugs or sex or travel. Jesus said, "People soon become thirsty again after drinking this water. But the water I give them takes away thirst altogether. It becomes a perpetual spring within them, giving them eternal life" (John 4:13–14 NLT).

You are very much like your neighbor who may not believe in Jesus Christ—you both become thirsty. The difference is that you know where to go to quench that thirst—"As the deer pants for streams of water, so I long for you, O God. I thirst for God, the living God" (Psalm 42:1–2).

Do you sometimes worry about how to testify of Christ to your thirsty neighbor? "What should I say? When should I say it?" Think about it in this way: Can't a thirsty person recognize someone who is satisfied? Yes. One of the best things you can do for your neighbor is satisfy your own thirst at the spring of living water that gives eternal life. How? In private prayer and singing, Bible reading and fellowship. Then pray that your friends will recognize their thirst as did the Samaritan woman at Jacob's well (see John 4:7–15). One day you may be surprised when someone asks you, "Give me this water, so that I may never be thirsty" (v. 15). Soon you will be rejoicing with them, singing, "Hallelujah! I have found him whom my soul so long has craved! Jesus satisfies my longings; through his blood I now am saved."

RELATED SCRIPTURE READING—*Isaiah 12:2–3*

Lord, I once was thirsty for you; but by your mercy I found you. And so deliver me from a judgmental attitude toward the people who have not yet tasted you, the living water. I ask for a heart of love and an impulse to pray for them. As you have had mercy on me, extend your mercy to those around me. Become in them a well of water springing up into eternal life.

Praise to the Lord, the Almighty

Praise to the Lord, the Almighty, the King of creation!
O my soul, praise him, for he is thy health and salvation!
All ye who hear, now to his temple draw near;
Praise him in glad adoration.

Praise to the Lord, Who o'er all things so wondrously reigneth,
Shelters thee under his wings, yea, so gently sustaineth!
Hast thou not seen how thy desires e'er have been
Granted in what he ordaineth?

Praise to the Lord, who doth prosper thy work and defend thee;
Surely his goodness and mercy here daily attend thee.
Ponder anew what the Almighty can do,
If with his love he befriend thee.

Praise to the Lord, O let all that is in me adore him!
All that hath life and breath, come now with praises before him.
Let the *Amen* sound from his people again,
Gladly for all we adore him.

Catherine Winkworth (1827-1878)—Translator

Deeply interested in educational and social problems, Winkworth was secretary of the English Association for the Promotion of Higher Education for Women in 1870, was governor of the Red Maids' School, Bristol, promoter of the Clifton High School for Girls, and a member of Cheltenham Ladies' College (1871). She is regarded by many as the best of the translators from the German.

In translating this hymn, Catherine Winkworth gave a beautiful gift to the church. She must always be included among the women hymnists because, more than any other person, she helped bring the German chorale tradition to the English-speaking world.

The hymn itself was written by Joachim Neander (1650–1680) who studied theology at Bremen University in Germany. While principal of the Reformed Grammar School in Düsseldorf (1674–1679), he enjoyed excursions to the secluded Düssel river valley, which was at that time a deep ravine with numerous caves, grottos, and waterfalls. It is possible that Neander wrote and sang his poems in this beautiful setting.

In the mid-nineteenth century, the cement industry began to quarry the limestone in the Düssel river valley; the narrow ravine became a wide valley and was given the name Neander Valley (in German: *Neanderthal*). In the summer of 1856, archeologists found ancient skeletal remains in the valley and named them Neanderthal man. So, Joachim Neander has the distinction of being the only hymnist with a fossil hominid as a namesake. Isn't the church's heritage rich and surprising?

As for Catherine Winkworth, she lived much of her life in Manchester, England, although the church has been forever enriched because she lived one year in Dresden, Germany. Around 1854, she published *Lyra Germanica*, a book of German hymns translated into English. Winkworth went on to publish another series of German hymns in 1858; in 1863, she issued *The Chorale Book for England*, and in 1869, *Christian Singers of Germany*. Thank God for Ms. Winkworth, who gave us access to the poetry and songs of the German Reformation!

RELATED SCRIPTURE READING—*Romans 16:1-23*

O God, you alone are my inheritance, my cup of blessing. You guard all that is mine. The land you have given me is a pleasant land. What a wonderful inheritance! I am thankful you did not take that awful cup from Jesus. He drank it to the bottom. So I drink the cup of blessing with all those I have inherited as my brothers and sisters in your family.

'Tis So Sweet to Trust in Jesus

'Tis so sweet to trust in Jesus, just to take him at his word;
Just to rest upon his promise; just to know, thus saith the Lord.

Jesus, Jesus, how I trust him, how I've proved him o'er and o'er,
Jesus, Jesus, precious Jesus! O for grace to trust him more.

O how sweet to trust in Jesus, just to trust his cleansing blood;
Just in simple faith to plunge me, 'neath the healing, cleansing flood.

Yes, 'tis sweet to trust in Jesus, just from sin and self to cease;
Just from Jesus simply taking life and rest, and joy and peace.

I'm so glad I learned to trust him, precious Jesus, Savior, friend;
And I know that he is with me, will be with me to the end.

Louisa M. R. Wodehouse (1850-1917)

A little girl, age nine, in Dover, England, decided she wanted to be a foreign missionary. Her name was Louisa. At age twenty-one, at a camp meeting in Ohio, she offered herself for the mission field but was rejected because of her frail health. She married and had a daughter. After her husband drowned while trying to save a life in the surf off Long Island, Louisa and her daughter went to South Africa where they served fifteen years as missionaries. There she married Robert Wodehouse. He became a Methodist minister, and in 1901 they went to a Methodist mission in Southern Rhodesia (now Zimbabwe). Louisa Wodehouse served the Lord there until her death.

*J*ob said, "Have I put my trust in money or felt secure because of my gold? Does my happiness depend on my wealth and all that I own? . . . it would mean I had denied the God of heaven" (Job 31:24, 28 NLT).

Some two thousand years later Jesus said very much the same thing: "Real life is not measured by how much we own. . . . A person is a fool to store up earthly wealth but not have a rich relationship with God" (Luke 12:15, 21).

Nearly two thousand years again passed and C. S. Lewis wrote in *Mere Christianity:* "One of the dangers of having a lot of money is that you may be quite satisfied with the kinds of happiness money can give and so fail to realize your need for God. If everything seems to come simply by signing checks, you may forget that you are at every moment totally dependent on God."

Today, success is measured in coarsely materialistic terms. Politics, business, and personal wealth are foremost concerns in American society. Sadly this measure of success has crept into the church. So there is a desperate need of people to pray in the pattern of Ephesians 1—"I pray for you constantly, asking God, . . . to give you spiritual wisdom and understanding, so that you might grow in your knowledge of God. I pray that your hearts will be flooded with light . . . *I want you to realize what a rich and glorious inheritance he has given to his people*" (vv. 16–18, italics added).

This is a prayer of Paul, who at the end of his life could say, "I know the one in whom I trust, and I am sure that he is able to guard what I have entrusted to him until the day of his return" (2 Timothy 1:12). A rich relationship with God is the eternal, invisible measure of success.

RELATED SCRIPTURE READING—*Matthew 6:25-34*

Dear God, whom have I in heaven but you? I desire you more than anything on earth. My health may fail, and my spirit may grow weak, but you remain the strength of my heart; you are mine forever. How good it is to be near you! I have made you my shelter. Thank you for all you are to me, Lord.

109

Index of Hymns and Tune Names

Most hymn tunes have been given a unique name. When a tune is included in a hymnal, its name can usually be found in an index to that hymnal. The names of the tunes most often used to accompany the lyrics found in *Women of Sacred Song* are provided here in parentheses following the hymn title.

111

Margaret and Daniel Partner live in Peacham, Vermont. Margaret is a church pianist, storyteller, and teacher. Daniel is an editor and writer whose projects include *Bedtime Bible Story Book, One Year Book of Personal Prayer,* and *Oswald Chambers Daily Devotional Bible.*